BILL RICHARDSON is a very popular an[...] writer who is also the host of the daily cu[...] *Richardson's Roundup* on CBC Radio One, broadcast weekdays across Canada from 2:06 to 4 PM (2:36 to 4:30 PM in Newfoundland). He and the show have been praised in the *The Rough Guide to Internet Radio*: "Richardson's music is drawn from all over to fit with the spoken material that makes up most of the *Roundup*: storytellers from across Canada mixed with liberal doses of listeners' letters and calls. What makes this all much more interesting than a description of it sounds is Richardson himself: his voice, his wit, and most of all his expansive spirit."

After winning the Stephen Leacock Medal for Humour for his first novel, the best-selling *Bachelor Brothers' Bed and Breakfast*, he wrote two more books in the series: *Bachelor Brothers' Bed and Breakfast Pillow Book* (winner of a B.C. Book Award) and *Bachelor Brothers' Bedside Companion*.

His other books include *Canada Customs*, *Queen of All the Dustballs*, *Guy to Goddess* (with photographer Rosamond Norbury), *Scorned & Beloved: Dead of Winter Meetings with Canadian Eccentrics*, *oddball@large* (a collection of his columns from various newspapers) and *After Hamelin* (a book for children).

Waiting for Gertrude, his most recent novel, was a finalist for the Leacock Award.

Bill Richardson lives in Vancouver with two dogs and a cat.

BILL RICHARDSON

Dear Sad Goat

A Roundup of Truly Canadian
Tales & Letters

Douglas & McIntyre
Vancouver / Toronto

Douglas & McIntyre
2323 Quebec Street, Suite 201
Vancouver, British Columbia V5T 4S7
www.douglas-mcintyre.com

National Library of Canada Cataloguing in Publication Data
Main entry under title:
    Dear Sad Goat
    Contributions from listeners of Richardson's roundup.
    ISBN 1-55054-960-X

1. Canada—Social life and customs—Anecdotes. 2. Canadian wit and humor (English).
3. Richardson's roundup (Radio program). I. Richardson, Bill, 1955– II. Richardson's roundup (Radio program)
FC89.D42 2002   971.0648'0'207   C2002-910830-6
F1021.2.D423 2002

Editing by Saeko Usukawa
Cover and text design by Jacqueline Verkley
Goat photographs by Rosamond Norbury
Drawings by Roxanna Bickadoroff
Printed and bound in Canada by Friesens
Printed on acid-free paper

The publisher gratefully acknowledges the financial support of the Canada Council for the Arts, the British Columbia Ministry of Tourism, Small Business and Culture, and the Government of Canada through the Book Publishing Industry Development Program (BPIDP) for its publishing activities.

> CONTENTS

To the Listeners and the Tellers

ABOUT "DEAR SAD GOAT"

Radio has two qualities that I admire above all others. The first—and this is deeply, embarrassingly Canadian—is its modesty. It doesn't matter how you gussy it up or how many bells and whistles you add with satellites or fibre optics, it doesn't matter whether you receive programs on a doddering clock radio or on a spiffy new laptop via the Internet, radio is now what it has always been and will always be: a faceless voice and perhaps some music that float for a second on the air, then are lost to the ether. Here is technology used laudably and blamelessly as the handmaid for an elemental human requirement: the need to tell and to hear stories.

I also appreciate that radio, for all its facelessness, is an intensely visual medium. The most obvious demonstration of this—and my on-air colleagues could all tell similar stories—occurs when I meet someone who listens but has never seen my mug, and who says, almost inevitably, "Oh! You don't look anything like you sound." Of course, this requires that I ask who or what they imagined I might be, and for the longest time I would hear, "I thought you'd be older and fatter." When, several years ago, these good souls stopped saying "older," I pretty much abandoned this line of inquiry.

Now, this story is meant not as an illustration of my vanity—although I guess it's also that—but rather to point out how radio discourages passivity in its audience by requiring their active participation. Unlike television, with its relentless parade of imposed visuals, radio engages the imagination by exciting our urge to create pictures: of the host or the news reader, of the events described in whatever narrative is on the air. However dumb it might be on any given day, radio still requires something of the brain that the visual media do not, and I believe instinctively that this is a good thing.

Richardson's Roundup, the program I've had the good luck to host for the past five years on CBC Radio 1, richly embodies these qualities of modesty and imagination. Certainly, it was designed with modesty—and with cost savings—in mind. It was the inspiration of Alex Frame, a veteran CBC producer and executive, now Vice-President of English Radio. In the spring of 1997, as head of English Radio Programming, Mr. Frame issued a call for proposals for a program that he had, in fact, already designed; a show to occupy the afternoon time slot that had long been the home of the talented and popular Vicki Gabereau, who was heading off to graze the more expensively manicured fields of television.

The show that Mr. Frame had invented, and on which he was inviting bids, was nothing like the generous mix of music, chat and lively interviews that had been Vicki's à la carte offering, five days a week. Rather, this was to be a program that would feature repeat broadcasts of other CBC radio shows, a "best of" amalgam, an aural alloy of interviews and features culled from here and there over the broadcast day. Mr. Frame's point, which was and remains a good one, is that many excellent features and documentaries are only heard once, and only by that segment of the population that happens to have an ear cocked to the crystal set at any given moment. So, why not give these fine works another airing?

Along with Tod Elvidge and Heather Kennedy, both CBC Radio producers of long standing and great distinction, I was able to make a case for a program that would feature a "blue box" component of eminently recyclable items, and a component that would be "audience driven": i.e., stories and musical requests solicited from our listeners. We proposed to ask for both letters and phone calls that would emphasize family and domestic tales rather than social or political commentary. Then, we would take all these various bits and somehow fold them into a savoury collation.

There was not, I freely confess, a single whiff of anything like originality about our plan. It had all been done before. As noted, we would not be generating any of our own interviews, and practically every radio show on the schedule used, still uses, audience feedback gathered in the usual ways: mail, E-mail, fax and phone. Why would they not? There is every good reason to make hay with what the audience sends, letters most particularly. That letters from CBC Radio listeners will be literate, thoughtful, funny, provocative, angry, informed, confessional or tender has become a given over the years. Anyone who ever listened to Peter Gzowski's *Morningside*, or to *Gabereau*, or to the summer series called *Crosswords*, has heard ample evidence that this is so, and we had no reason to suppose that it would be otherwise for the *Roundup*. The letters collected here are a clear demonstration that this confidence was not misplaced.

Right from the get-go, we could see that the stories told by our audience would become the heart of the show. That has not changed, although the *Roundup* has evolved and altered in many other ways over its five seasons. Most of our interviews, features and specials are now produced in-house, for example, and the show has developed its own particular quirks, idiosyncrasies, codes and signals. Most telling, perhaps, is the fact that almost no one who is a regular listener to the program calls it by its official name. Instead, it is now known, rather cultishly, as "Sad Goat." Why "Sad Goat" is the question I am most often asked, and I am happy to set the answer down here so that there will be a permanent record of this, sadly, rather prosaic story.

In order to encourage our listeners to tell their stories via the phone, and in order to spare them long-distance charges if they were calling from outside the Lower Mainland of British Columbia, we applied for and were assigned a toll-free line: 1-888-723-4628. If you scan the letters attached to those last seven numbers, you will see that they spell out the handy mnemonic RADIO 2 U. My original intention was to announce the number in just that way: "Call us now at 1-888-RADIO 2 U!" However, I then realized that there would be misunderstandings, that listeners would try to dial TO YOU, that endless explanations would be required, that I would always be footnoting the joke. Surely, I thought, there must be something more suitable. On investigation, I discovered that the letters attached to those numbers also spell out SAD GOAT, which means absolutely nothing, which is in no way germane, which has no bearing whatsoever on the matter at hand and, which is, of course, exactly what I liked about it. So, I shelved RADIO 2 U and opted for SAD GOAT.

Why listeners warmed to it so readily and to such an extent that "Sad Goat" became the *de facto* name of the program, I can't accurately say. However, I think it has something to do with those Canadian qualities of modesty and imagination. There's something endearing and unflashy about the idea of a goat—especially if you've never been involved in their rearing and husbandry—and a sad goat is all the more winning, in a modest, melancholic, unlikely way. You can't say or hear the words "sad goat" in tandem without imagining what such a creature looks like, or without wondering at the root cause of the sadness; and for this reason, if for no other, it is memorable. And perhaps there is something welcoming about a sad goat, something that suggests a ready ear, a giving heart and a willingness to take in confidences. Certainly, our audience has shown itself willing over the years to share its thoughts, feelings, truths and humour.

It was a great pleasure going back over files from the past five years, looking at the thousands of pieces of correspondence we have received. What you'll find here is a sample of 163 letters. A few have been written by listeners who are also writers, but mostly these are the everyday stories of everyday people who don't see their first job as the telling of stories but who do it extraordinarily well. The letters have not been arranged in order of receipt, nor have they been exactly organized according to themes, which is how they tend to come to us. Stories about getting stuck in unlikely places. Stories about pianos. Stories about meeting the in-laws, about who taught you to tie a tie or bake a pie, about weddings and child-rearing and graves and gravy and scars and cars. I've taken samples from some of the dozens of topics that have evolved and picked letters that somehow dovetail into or fold out of each other, one leading to the next, in the same weirdly circuitous, perversely logical way that each day's show is organized.

These are all good letters, though not necessarily the best of the best. They have been chosen because they fit well, one with another, and give a sense of the Sad Goat thus far; at least, the letter component of the program. Ironically, I have not included any of the tens of thousands of phone calls made to 1-888-SAD GOAT since the fall of 1997. In my estimation, these just didn't sing on the page in the same way they do on the airwaves. There are also other gaps that regular listeners to the *Roundup* will surely notice, and, I imagine, regret. Not included here, for reasons only of brute practicality, are such memorable tales as those told by Elizabeth Creith, our shepherd in residence, or by Micheal Vonn, who wrote about her experiences at law school, or the stories Nancy Angermeyer has written from Saturna Island about her goat Milli, whose life has been hugely eventful and who won the contest to become the *Roundup*'s "spokesgoat." It's Milli's face you see on the cover of this book, and that's also her on the back, bussing me on the ear.

When I look at that picture—taken, as you will note, when I was going through a phase of helping the blond along—I remember vividly the day I spent on Saturna with several CBC colleagues and photographer Rosamond Norbury, all of us enjoying the hospitality of Nancy Angermeyer and her partner, Richard Blagborne. It was spring and more than a little damp, and we were there, among other things, to take the photographs that would be used on our T-shirts, postcards and other such tchotchkes. I talk a lot about goats, but the truth is that, until then, my hands-on experience of them had been limited to the odd visit at a petting zoo. Milli, I was told by everyone who is in a position to know, is a very sweet goat. Nonetheless, she didn't demonstrate a tremendous willingness to remain calm, neutral and poised while Rosamond did her work. Various blandishments and bribes were offered up, and the goat-kissing picture was finally taken while the wind was blowing and the rain was falling and I was being anointed with milk—goat's milk—so that Milli would have a focus other than my waning pulchritude. There have not been many occasions over the course of my *Roundup* career when I have felt myself entering a dark night of the soul, but that, I don't mind telling you, was one of them.

I would like to thank everyone who has taken the time to phone or write to share their stories with our audience, and to acknowledge the generosity of those listeners whose letters are included in *Dear Sad Goat*. Royalties from the book's sale will be divided between two fund-raising efforts, one on the east coast and one on the west. A portion of the proceeds will be directed to Saturna Island Elementary School, where Milli the goat is a well-known visitor. Like most small, rural schools, Saturna Elementary faces many challenges, and the money will be used to sustain school programs and for the bursary fund. The other recipient of the royalties will be the St. John's Restoration Fund (you can visit their Web site at www.stjohnsrestoration.com). St. John's Church, in Lunenburg, Nova Scotia, was built in 1754. It was destroyed by fire on November 1, 2001. Amy Bennet, from Big Lots, Nova Scotia, near Lunenburg, wrote a moving letter, which has been included in this collection, about the destruction of that landmark and its devastating effect on the community. Such a loss is not localized. Lunenburg is a UNESCO World heritage Site, and that lovely old church, one of Canada's most outstanding examples of Gothic carpenter architecture, really belong to us all, regardless of creed or location.

My thanks as well to Karin Konstantynowicz, a colleague for many years, who diligently tracked down the contributors to *Dear Sad Goat*, and to Saeko Usukawa, for her keen eye and steady editorial hand. Finally, and most particularly, I would like to thank my colleagues, whose dedication and inspiration make the *Roundup* a daily possibility, and whose ideas are everywhere in this book. Many, many producers, technicians and hosts have contributed to the show, directly and indirectly, in Vancouver and elsewhere. I thank them all, and would name them all, save for the risks of carelessly overlooking someone and giving offence, and because such a list would be very long and unwieldy. However, I am particularly indebted to a core group of colleagues, without whom, it can truly be said, there would never be a *Roundup*: Rosemary Allenbach, Ross Bragg, Tod Elvidge, Paul Grant, Andrea Hunter, Sheryl MacKay, Marc Murray, Sheila Peacock, Damiano Pietropaolo, Marie-Helene Robitaille, Aynsley Vogel, and, most especially, our remarkable and very hard-working executive producer, Heather Kennedy.

PART 1

BECAUSE YOU TOLD ME HE WAS DEAD

If you were to believe the papers or the newscasts, you'd wind up thinking that our society's agenda is, first and foremost, political and economic. I would never discount the importance of the Big Issues or dismiss the need for their reporting, but I don't think they're what powers us along or fuels our engines. Politicians come and go. Markets rise and fall. Headlines scream the news of dire catastrophes, and within a week or two the tailings of whatever explosion, quake or tornado will turn up at the bottom of the back pages. This is predicable. This is cyclical. We know that this will happen, just as it has happened before.

And the whole while that the world is churning up what will either be forgotten or will one day be known as history, we keep living our own small lives: lives that bring us into contact with our friends, neighbours, co-workers and family members who are, likewise, living their own small lives. Out of that contact comes a constant flow of narrative: the small stories of small lives that are completely overlooked by the brokers of what we call "The News." And are they any the less important because of that? Not in my books, friend. Not in my books. Those stories are the Roundup's bread and butter, stories that are domestic, often comic, well-loved and well-practised family tales. They tend to be variations on the theme of: Everything was going along just fine, and then... As the following letters demonstrate, that ellipsis accommodates a tremendous variety.

Last year, one frosty morning in January, with the temperature hovering around minus 25, my dog and I took our usual early morning walk down to the lake. The cold had kept all the fishermen off the ice, but there was a funny lump lying a few feet off shore. As I got nearer, I saw it was a boot, but, to my horror, it was also attached to a leg, and I found myself staring at a motionless body lying face down in the snow. Nipper was delighted to have someone on his level and immediately tried to stick his nose down the lifeless ear.

I called off Nipper and ran back to the house, yelling to my husband that there was a dead body on the ice. I phoned the ambulance and some neighbours while Bill went to help. I grabbed some blankets just in case and went back outside. I couldn't believe my eyes. Everyone was standing around, and they were actually laughing, and there was no body in sight.

Of course, all the ice fishermen out there knew that the "body" was a fisherman just looking down the hole. He was watching a fish that was just about to take the bait. He knew we were both there but was scared that if he moved he would spook the fish. He said that he looked up to see me running down the road and thought to himself, "She must be late for an appointment."

By this time, we could hear the siren of the approaching ambulance and everyone, including even my dog, vanished into thin air, leaving me standing all alone in the middle of the road to face an incredulous ambulance crew.

Later, Bill told me that he had seen the body on the ice when he had his shower. I asked rather hotly why he had let me go to the lake with a body on it. He replied, "I thought he was just looking down the hole."

I positively howled, "Then why didn't you tell me that?"

To which he replied, "Because you told me was dead."

I think I also made some comment about the fact that in the civilized world, where I came from, people did not go about lying face down in the snow at minus 25 for fun.

As you can imagine, this story will go down in the local folklore of the area. My only defence is that in every book I've read, it is always the person walking their dog in the morning mist, down by the water, who trips over the dead body. I figured it was my turn.

> CECILE PRATT, IOO MILE HOUSE, BRITISH COLUMBIA

She put it into the bathtub. Now, in most cases, something in the bathtub is nothing unusual, but this something splashed occasionally. It all started one sunny cold winter day in my home province of Alberta. My mother had decided that it was a fine day to die for some fish, so off she went to the not-so-local Pigeon Lake, where she had fished many times to the culinary delight of our family. But this turned out to be a very different occasion. After catching her limit and heading home, it was time to clean fish, and, much to her dismay, there was a live fish in the bottom of the black plastic garbage bag where she had placed her bounty.

Now, my mother has never been one to "dispose" of one of nature's creatures recklessly, but her unflappable logic still makes me smile years later. Since the fish had survived being hooked, dragged from its watery home and hauled in a plastic bag with only the melting ice to keep it alive for several hours, it deserved to live; and so she put it into the bathtub overnight, where I discovered it when I used the toilet the next morning. A shock to say the least, but there was one fish that had a 40-mile ride back to its home, where my mother drilled a hole in the ice and very carefully slipped the fish back into the lake.

> CAROL BOUCHER, COBBLE HILL, BRITISH COLUMBIA

In 1955, when I was a student in London, England, I met and fell in love with a young woman who lived with her parents in Newcastle, some 450 kilometres north. The only way I could afford to visit her was to hitchhike up the overcrowded, twisting, pre-motorway roads on Friday evenings—returning on Sunday night by the same method. It was a journey that took between seven and twelve hours each way. When I arrived at my destination in the small hours of the morning, I slept on the couch until the family got moving about.

The girl's father did not take kindly to my attentions. For a start, I was a southerner, so couldn't be trusted; and secondly, what sane, reasonable human being would willingly give up two nights' sleep over the weekend just to spend time with a member of the opposite sex? The atmosphere was as frosty as the North of England winter. Communications between us were conducted through his wife, who was kind enough to tell me whenever I was putting the wrong foot forward.

The man of the house was a hard worker who worked overtime every Saturday. He would get up at six, and his wife would prepare breakfast. He would be out of the door by quarter to seven, and his wife would return to bed for a couple of hours.

After a few weeks of my visits, I was informed through the official channels that I was not to use the bathroom on my arrival, because the sound of the flush disturbed the breadwinner. I was to wait until he had left for work—a small, if somewhat uncomfortable sacrifice for the sake of harmony with my future father-in-law. So, the next weekend, after arriving at 3 AM, I waited until I heard the front door close and was sure that his wife had returned to bed before leaping happily into the toilet. It was the only toilet in the house.

This was nearly fifty years ago, so the toilet had a chain attached to the cistern overhead. The room was tiny, just wide enough for the equipment and one occupant. On the wall next to the toilet was a cast-iron toilet-roll holder, a simple bar that stuck out at a convenient height.

Having done what I had to do, I pulled on the chain. The chain broke, but my arm continued its descent and struck the toilet-roll holder. The holder came away from the wall and began its fall to earth. With space so limited, the toilet bowl was in direct line with the descending cast-iron bracket. I watched as the heavy metal bracket—seemingly in slow motion—struck the bowl, which exploded with a terrific bang into a thousand fragments. There was nothing left of it but a jagged hole in the floor. I was horror-stricken.

It is, I think, to my credit that I didn't put on my coat there and then and get back on the southbound road, never to return. It is a terrifying thing to be eighteen years old and to have to wake the mother of your girlfriend to tell her that you have single-handedly done more damage to her facilities than the Germans managed to do with all their bombing a few years earlier.

But worse was to follow. Her husband liked to come home for lunch, and, being a fastidious man, he did not like to use the washrooms at the factory where he worked. He looked forward, I was informed, to a few minutes of peace and quiet in this tiny room where he could be alone with his thoughts while his wife put his lunch on the table. So I was instructed to go down to his workplace and tell him that he had better go at the factory, because there was nowhere for him to go at home.

How was I going to phrase it? How do you tell a man who doesn't really want to acknowledge your existence that you have done something like this? The ten-minute walk went too fast. I was at the factory gate long before I was ready.

I was ushered into the foreman's office. The man was sent for. What he thought, I cannot imagine. He might first have been expecting a reprimand or a commendation from his foreman. Seeing me in the office, he must have realized that some disaster had befallen his household. The sheer magnitude of the disaster could not have been imagined. It was, I am quite sure, the most harrowing interview I have ever had: on my side, it was conducted in a falsetto voice at very high speed—on his, it was conducted in a series of grunts through very tight lips. The foreman smirked in the background.

Anyway, it all turned out okay in the end. He remodelled the bathroom to include quite a spacious area for a modern toilet. I married his daughter, and we have remained married for forty-two years.

> RAY WILL, ST. PHILIPS, NEWFOUNDLAND

Some years ago, I was travelling on a bus in Manchester, England. On the seat in front of me were a little lad and his mother. The mother kept saying, "I'll give you Dick Barton," in an angry voice, accompanying the remark with a shove. This was in the pre-television days, when the BBC broadcast every weekday evening an extremely popular radio serial about a special agent named Dick Barton (and his colleagues Jock and Snowy). Each episode ended in a cliff-hanger and was so entrancing that, once, a group of kids hired a taxi to take them to Broadcasting House to help rescue him from his latest predicament. The unhappy-looking lad was wearing a Balaclava helmet, and there was a huge bulge sticking out where his ear should be.

In Manchester, people talk to strangers, so I asked the mother what was going on. She whipped off the Balaclava, saying, "I'll give him Dick Barton." Inverted on his head was an enamel "potty," and melted butter was running down his face. She explained that he had been playing Dick Barton with his brother and had put on the potty as a helmet. His brother had bashed him on the top with a cricket bat, forcing it down over his forehead. They had turned him upside down and poured in melted butter to no avail, and they were on their way to the hospital to have it removed.

The butter had had some effect—you could take hold of the handle and spin it round. Most of the passengers took turns at doing this, and all except the mother and son thought it was very amusing. I still do!

> DON ATKINSON, RICHMOND, ONTARIO

I grew up on a tiny farm outside a town of twenty-four people, 100 miles south of Winnipeg. One summer day, when the temperature was around 100 degrees, I was mowing hay about 4 miles from home. The tractor blew a hose, and I was instantaneously drenched from head to toe with hot oil. I began the long walk home for help.

My spirits lifted when I passed a beautiful, blooming yellow sea of sunflowers. Unfortunately, I frightened up what seemed like a million red-winged blackbirds that were feeding on the seeds. With a furious flurry of flapping, they burst from the field like an explosion and exited right over my head, passing everything they had ever known—literally! On top of my oil and sweat, I now was blessed with the sogginess and smelliness of a thousand blackbird stool specimens.

I had reached my limit. There was nothing else I could do. I guffawed the final 2 miles home, and, as soon as my mother saw me, she did, too. That's the closest I've ever come to being tarred and feathered!

> TERRY RUUD, MOOREHEAD, MINNESOTA

In the '70s, we moved to a farm: back-to-the-landers looking for a clean environment and a peaceful setting where we could raise our children. The garden came first; a third of an acre of vegetables nurtured by our own blistered hands. Chickens arrived next; first a dozen layers, then 150 chicks, which we raised to a dressed weight of 4 to 6 kilos. We butchered and eviscerated them ourselves and sold them to friends who appreciated organically fed meat. Then we graduated to pigs.

We started with three and kept two to breed with Boris, a prize boar. In late winter, when he detected signs of labour, my husband moved a sleeping bag into the barn and reviewed the birthing instructions for piglets as explained in *Harrowsmith* magazine. The two sows waited until my husband returned to the house for a meal and delivered themselves of a total of twenty-one piglets.

In the fall, when the twenty-one pigs were ready to make their final journey to the abattoir, my husband was away on a long business trip. A long-suffering friend agreed to help me corral the pigs and load them onto the livestock-removal truck. We thought we were clever, herding the pigs into a narrow aisle of the barn and, indeed, getting their co-operation at this initial stage was easy. We assumed that we could simply force them onto the truck by blocking the aisle with our bodies as we moved to decrease the space between the pigs and the back of the truck. We were wrong. A pig has no loose flesh to grab onto. A pig has no neck around which to tie a rope. It is a solid, dense mass of strength and determination.

As time passed, the floor grew slippery with a greasy combination of urine and manure. We slid and slipped and often lost our balance in our attempts to gain the co-operation of the pigs. The process took two hours of trial and error, until we discovered that we could grab the tail and a hind leg to steer each pig in the direction we chose. In the end, we were completely soaked in pig excrement, but by this time our nostrils had been fairly desensitized to the aroma and we could laugh at our sorry state of dishevelment.

We hosed ourselves off outside and went off to our respective tubs. The clothes we had worn had to be bagged and discarded. Even after several soaks and scrubs, I still smelled pig. And I was not alone. When I went to school the next day, my students were not at all subtle about informing me that I was not a rosebud. One boy spoke for them all: "I don't mean to be disrespectful, Mrs. A., but you stink. Then he laughed and said, "I've always wanted to say that to a teacher."

Well, he should have been around the year my husband shot the skunk on our porch and the smell oozed into the house. Then there was the time, before we had a truck, when I loaded the goat into the back seat of the Duster and took her to visit the buck down the road. But that's another story.

> TANYA AMBROSE, MALLORYTOWN, ONTARIO

M y four siblings and I grew up in southwestern Ontario on a beef farm. One beautiful afternoon in late August, we were ready to go to the local fall fair, when somebody noticed that some steers had escaped the barnyard, and one of them had fallen into the liquid manure pit.

"Quick, get the loader!" was my father's cry. By "loader" he meant the hydraulic device mounted on a tractor and used for—you guessed it—loading solid manure into the manure spreader. Unfortunately, by the time the loader got to the scene, the poor animal had drowned.

The next thing Dad announced was that the steer was just about ready for market and was too valuable to go to waste. Now, no abattoir will take a dead steer for human consumption. For one thing, you have to drain the blood very quickly before it coagulates. But Dad had a plan. He instructed me to lift him in the bucket of the loader over the liquid manure pit, so that he could get a chain around the steer. In no time, we had the beast on dry land, and Dad was ordering us to take it up to the barn to hose it off.

"I'm going to the house to get Mum's big knife," he announced. I was horrified. I'm not sure if it was the prospect of the job which obviously lay ahead or the missing of the fall fair after getting especially cleaned up. In the end, we all pitched in, and by dark we had our next year's supply of beef stowed in our ancient freezer. I seem to remember that we actually made it to the fair that evening.

As you may have guessed, there is more. About three days later, we noticed a strange smell in the house. Investigation revealed that our ancient freezer was OK for storing already frozen stuff but definitely not OK for cooling down

15

500 or 600 pounds of hot stuff! Once again, Dad was adamant that this valuable steer was not going to go to total waste. So we spent a memorable afternoon sorting the good meat from the bad. Everybody except for Dad was very sceptical, but he said that he would be the tester and have the first meal. Once we got over the thought of it, we discovered that actually it was the best beef we ever had! We called it our pre-aged beef.

> KEN HUMPHREY, IONA STATION, ONTARIO

On my parents' farm in Cardigan, Prince Edward Island, we have always had animals that were destined for the freezer and eventually the table. The animals included, over the years, chickens, pigs, cows, goats and ducks.

This October, I was getting married. My parents wanted to contribute to the wedding in some manner, and it was decided that they would provide the beef for my wedding meal. Now, I don't call the cows by name; I rarely spend time in the barn. I think the cow used for the wedding beef was named Bert. The day my father took Bert to the butcher shop, somebody jokingly told me that I should take a picture. I did, and I've included the picture in my album of "pre-wedding" photos.

I am pleased to know that the beef for my wedding was provided with love from my parents and that I know how the beef was raised. In preparing his speech for my wedding, Dad considered opening with a joke about what a good meal Bert made. After some consideration, he decided to just remain silent about the whole thing so as to prevent any guest from getting upset.

> MARY BEAULAC, CORNWALL, PRINCE EDWARD ISLAND

A few years ago, I was returning to Red Deer, Alberta, after a job interview in Calgary. It was an uneventful trip, and I was on the outskirts of Red Deer when I came up behind a pickup truck pulling a stock trailer. I noticed that the trailer door was not securely closed. I decided that perhaps I should back off somewhat, and no sooner had I done so than the trailer door was flung open and the back end of a cow materialized in the doorway. In what is perhaps the most surreal moment of my life, the cow proceeded to fall out backwards, followed by three of its brethren.

They tumbled and cartwheeled on the asphalt in my direction, like so many leather-clad boulders. They must have fallen on their flanks for, miraculously, none of them seemed to have broken their legs. Once they had finally come to a stop, three of the cows got up and staggered into the grass at the side of the road. One cow, however, was not going to have any of that. It continued to stagger down the road. It evoked images reminiscent of the running of the bulls in Pamplona when the bulls have hit the restraining walls a few too many times. Traffic had picked up, and, with the safety of the cow and oblivious drivers in mind, I remained behind this cow with my emergency flashers on. The cow, however, was a courteous road occupant. It travelled in the right direction and kept to the slow lane. Finally, after about 200 metres, the cow finally had enough and ran off into the ditch.

I later considered what had happened and surmised that I had narrowly avoided a horrific fate. The horror avoided was not merely my potential death but, rather, becoming the butt of jokes about how too much red meat can kill you.

> BOB NICHOLSON, RED DEER, ALBERTA

Waverley Elementary School in southeast Edmonton was, and presumably still is, a beautiful school, Frank Lloyd Wright–esque in design, with lots of open beams and common spaces. It was there that I fell under the influence of a certain Master Kevin Brown. He was probably the tallest kid in the school and certainly the weirdest. He was also brilliant—a fact confirmed all through elementary, junior and senior high and most likely the reason that spared him from the cruelty of the cooler elementary school thugs. He made me a co-conspirator in his drill of favour, which was to bottle, inventory and, ultimately, deliver imaginary milk all around the schoolyard. Each recess bell signalled play time, smoke time, time to get the bejesus beat out of you for most kids; but for us, it was the signal that our shift had begun.

Silverwood was the dairy we "worked" for, and an imaginary taskmaster named "Mr. Al" was our supervisor. Child labour laws did not apply in our schoolyard. We had fifteen minutes, twice a day, to get the cow juice out. Five days a week, we would deliver Silverwood milk to the portables, to the monkey bars, to each window of the school. We never actually delivered to another student or teacher. That would make us look crazy.

This was no small-time fantasy. We had milk trucks, we had a bottling operation complete with real milk caps that got pretty funky in the hot spring sun, and we had inventory lists and intercoms etched into the chocolate brown paint of the portables. Yes, we were weirdos, but we were do-good weirdos, bringing calcium to the people.

This went on for a couple of years until either the cow died or I thought the imaginary play of my childhood was too gooberish even for me. Kevin continued to deliver invisible milk for another couple of years. I think I pretended not to know him, but once, I was just like him. For all I know, good old Kevin Brown may be living our elementary-school dream today, as home-delivered milk has become so in vogue again. I hope he found joy in his life; he certainly helped me march to the beat of my own drummer, and no, despite all of this, I am not lactose-intolerant.

> MURRAY BILIDA, VANCOUVER, BRITISH COLUMBIA

My son asked me to look after his young children while he and his wife took a much-needed weekend away. The youngest child was seven months old and nursing. In the week prior to the parents leaving, the mother managed to extract several bottles of her breast milk to cover the baby's needs while she was absent. So food was not the problem. The manner of presentation was. I picked up the baby and, with much cooing and sweet talk, presented the bottle. As soon as the baby saw that plastic nipple, she clamped her jaws shut. Her lips stayed sealed until either her anger or her hunger became unbearable. When she opened her mouth to howl, I quickly inserted the offending nipple. After a few desperate sucks, she'd spit out the thing and resume her howling.

Her three-year-old sister followed me around all day, scowling at my inefficiency, enumerating her own many needs. By evening, we were all exhausted.

"I'll sleep with you," the three year old announced, as I got her ready for bed. "The baby might wake up and need me." So, while I undressed, she sat on my bed waiting and watching. As I dropped my nightie over my head, she demanded, "Gran, why do you wear those things if there isn't any milk in them?"

> LAUREL BAIRD, NANAIMO, BRITISH COLUMBIA

When I was breast-feeding my third baby, my mother said to me: "You nursed your other two babies; you can't expect a lot of milk will be left for this one." It was her theory that a woman came with "X" gallons of milk, with each nursling drinking a portion of it.

I explained the law of supply and demand to her, but I didn't convince her. She made a similar comment when I was nursing my fourth (and last) baby.

> GRACE LILIAN DARNEY, NEW WESTMINSTER, BRITISH COLUMBIA

Twenty-three years ago this month, I was close to nine months pregnant with our first son, David, when a life insurance salesman called to arrange an appointment.

This was fine. After all, we were looking forward to the responsibility of being parents, and it seemed that now was as good a time as any to take care of those vague and frightening details we'd been putting off for so long: financial planning, extra life insurance, a will.

The man arrived that evening, enthusiastic, bright and fresh-faced, made a beeline for our living room, opened up his large briefcase full of documents, and began his pitch. Our questions seemed to distract him from the script he'd rehearsed, but we continued to ask. What exactly were the differences between term and whole life? Could we use this as savings? His answers were a dog's breakfast of insurance bafflegab and always ended with, "And so, if you'll just sign here..."

My husband and I began to exchange looks across the room. If we were buying insurance, it wasn't going to be from this man. One of us—I can't remember who—began to end this ordeal with "Thank you very much for your time..." when we were interrupted.

"You're pregnant, I see."

"Yes, I am," I replied. "I'm due in about a week."

"Good, good. Are you nervous?"

"A little. Sure. It's our first, and I really don't know what to expect."

"Exactly!" He was excited now. "Exactly! This is why you need this policy. You could die in childbirth. This child could be without a mother, this man without a wife. In a week, you could very well be dead!" He raised his arm in a flourish, as though, with these words, he had clinched the deal.

In less than a minute, he was outside. We watched him from the window struggling to close the briefcase and put on the coat we had handed him as we helped him find his way out the door.

> LORRI NEILSEN GLENN, HUBBARDS, NOVA SCOTIA

As a nurse, I have sometimes taught prenatal classes. One group of eager learners was screening a birthing video. All appeared to be going well, until one young couple saw the actual birth. Howls, tears and great thumping of chests followed. They were hysterical. I had to remove them from the group. They asked me over and over if this was a real birth. I nodded, and they proceeded to wail and thump their chests again.

I asked them what was most disturbing to them, at which point the husband blurted out that their families had told them that babies enter the world flat and inflate once they hit the air.

I will say it took everything in me not to have a giggle at that moment. I reassured them and sent them on their way with more videos to view at home.

> CLAIRE LAWRENCE, PORT MOODY, BRITISH COLUMBIA

My husband's theory regarding the expansion of a pregnant woman's stomach, which he shared with me when I was pregnant with our first son, was that the extra skin required to allow for growth was carefully stored inside the navel. As the stomach expanded, the extra skin unwound from the navel.

> BECKY BLAIR, CRESTON, BRITISH COLUMBIA

I am a city girl, but every summer my family went to spend a week at the 127 Mile House ranch in the Cariboo in the central interior of British Columbia. My great-grandparents had homesteaded there in the late 1800s. I loved it there because I was nutty about horses. I have only one horrible memory of that time. It still causes me to shiver.

When I was about five, my job was to gather eggs from the chicken coop. I learned to make sure the rooster was at the back side of the coop behind the nesting boxes before I snuck in and loaded up my basket. One day, I mustn't have checked carefully enough on his whereabouts. Probably, I was thinking how nice I looked in my new top. I called it a "Mary Ann top," because it was red and white gingham, just like the tops worn by Mary Ann on *Gilligan's Island*. It left my tummy bare.

As I was carefully taking the last egg, the rooster jumped into the nesting box area and came toward me. I was terrified. I tried to run, but he lunged for my leg. I moved to the back of the coop again, hoping he would stay where he was. All the hens were in an uproar by now. I finally got up my resolve and rushed past him for the door. I moved faster and faster, thinking the sheer speed of my passage would make him back off. No such luck. He arched his neck out and pecked me hard right in the belly button. I cannot tell you how much it hurt. I cried for ages.

The two enduring lessons I got from the experience were: never mess with a nasty rooster and Band-Aids do not work on belly buttons.

> LORI WILLIAMS, VANCOUVER, BRITISH COLUMBIA

At seven, I attended Nicky Stroud's birthday party. It was the mid-1970s, and we were nine small girls, uniformly decked out in ruffled, flowery, puffed-sleeve long party frocks. Nicky's family lived in a wee white cottage at the bottom of a steep hill. It was surrounded by the towering eucalyptus and giant ferns of the Dandenong Ranges, which are situated outside metropolitan Melbourne. We tumbled through fern gullies to visit the "magic tree" where the elves lived as cockatoos squawked in trees far overhead.

After lunch, with two old bicycles between the ten of us, we were to race, in pairs, down the precipitous gravel road leading to the cottage. My turn was shared with Maree. Maree had been dropped on her head when an infant, and, something having been knocked loose, she blinked constantly. Halfway down the hill, I either hit a stone or the hem of my dress caught in the chain, or both. I sailed over the handlebars, flailing madly, with my chin stuck out defiantly. It took the brunt of my impact with the road.

I staggered back up the hill to where Maree had stopped her bike. My chin was a pulpy, bloody mess, gravel firmly embedded in raw flesh. Tears, blood and snot, which always runs freely with some people, especially crying children, dripped onto my party frock. The crowd at the foot of the hill had ceased its whoops and cheers. The forest had fallen eerily silent. Maree, too, was silent, and stared at me in horror, ever blinking, blinking, blinking. I had *killed* Nicky Stroud's birthday party.

My mother was watching from the kitchen window as Mr. Stroud's car pulled up outside and a bloodied little creature with a smashed-in chin was deposited on the curb. She continued to watch as he sped away with nary a word of apology or explanation, as I tottered across the front lawn in a daze.

The next day at school, when the entire teaching body had gathered in the staff room for morning tea, my mother, the school secretary, delivered against Mr. Stroud, a fourth-grade teacher, a bruising tirade about parental responsibility, gentlemanliness, good breeding and the value of a timely apology. As to the complete absence of scarring, my mother, the spitfire, had an unwavering faith in the healing powers of vitamin E cream. Every day before school and before bed at night, and on twice-daily visits to her office at school, Mom would slather my fast-healing disfigurement with her soothing balm. Some twenty-six years later, I still go through life with an unmarred chin thrust defiantly forward.

> TERESA LAWSON-WHEELER, CALGARY, ALBERTA

My first swimming lessons began at the age of five in Melbourne, Australia. This was in the late '30s. Each winter Saturday morning, some of my friends and their parents crammed into a Sunbeam Talbot and drove to the City Baths. The Sunbeam Talbot was a magnificent roadster. It had extra seats that folded into the back like a London taxi, and eight or nine could sit comfortably.

I loved Miss Lola Scott, our teacher. She taught swimming at the baths through the '30s and '40s with her sister, Peta. One by one, she gave us lessons wearing wooden clogs rather like early Dr. Scholl's. She carried a long bamboo pole with a huge hoop made of sailcloth at the end. Miss Scott clattered up and down the side of the pool, holding us up gently with the hoop as we struggled with our crawl, backstroke, breaststroke, side stroke. She taught us to dive off the side of the pool, hooking our chubby thumbs together. She counted our rhythm with a lovely, comforting, resonant voice. To assist us with our flutter kick, she'd sometimes intone rhythmically, "Mary, Mary, quite contrary, how does your garden grow?"

Lola Scott had won a state beauty contest. She was a Miss Victoria in the early '30s. She had attended the Berlin Olympic Games with her husband, Australian diving champion Arthur Morris. Lola Scott was beautiful, buxom, muscular and had huge green eyes. She was kind, refined and warm, and would occasionally hop into the pool with us. She seemed huge to us five year olds in her tight bathing cap and shiny racing Speedo bathing suit.

The small 24-foot ladies' pool had a little waterfall at one end. Small cubicles lined the sides, and near the showers at the deep end there was a wondrous machine. As a special treat, we could insert a penny into the machine and it would belch forth chocolate-covered peanuts into our little hands.

Sometimes I had swimming lessons after school. My mother and I would walk along Swanston Street to the station on the way home and detour slightly through Chinatown. There, my mother would buy me a magic flower that opened like a minute water lily when put into a glass of water. I remember staring through the doorways of Chinatown in those days and seeing people lying on couches taking opium.

The Melbourne City Baths is a magnificent Victorian building that, I'm happy to say, has been preserved and restored. A couple of years ago, I revisited the baths after about sixty years. The cubicles, the waterfall, the showers, everything was still there looking exactly the same, minus the peanut machine.

I still swim about four times a week and as I churn up and down the pool with excellent style and versatility I think about the Sunbeam Talbot, the chocolate-covered peanuts, the magic Chinese flowers and Chinatown. Most of all, I thank Lola Scott with her clogs, her bamboo pole, her green eyes and her kindness in those magic Melbourne winters of the '30s.

> BETH MARCILIO, TORONTO, ONTARIO

My partner, Charlie, and I moved to Ottawa from Sydney, Australia, in July 2000. A month or so before we left Australia, Charlie's father, Colin, offered him a coat for the chilly northern winter. It was the coat that Colin had worn in Scotland in the late '50s, when he was completing his Ph.D. in the cold and wet clime of Aberdeen.

We had never seen the coat—there not being much use for it in Sydney— and the offer was made over the phone from Colin's home three hours away, so there was no immediate chance to view it. Terrible visions came to our minds; Colin is not a man of sartorial elegance. Charlie mumbled a few feeble diverting remarks and said we'd see about it when we visited them before we left for Canada.

To our great grief, Charlie never saw his father alive again. Two weeks before we left for Canada, Colin died suddenly of a heart attack. There was no warning; he had been a very healthy, active seventy year old.

Now, Charlie has the coat with him here in Ottawa, and it is, to our surprise, very beautiful. It is long, charcoal grey and made of fine quality wool. It had been kept carefully by Colin for nearly forty years and is in mint condition. Its weight hangs reassuringly on one's shoulders. Charlie still harbours the regret that he did not accept his father's gift gratefully when it was offered—there can be so many regrets when someone dies—but the comfort in that coat and the knowledge that Colin kept warm in it as a young man keeps close to us many wonderful memories of Charlie's much-loved Dad.

> BRIDGET GROUNDS, OTTAWA, ONTARIO

When I was twenty, I set off on my first big journey, to live with a dairy farm family whom I did not know on the North Island of New Zealand. I milked four hundred cows in the Waikato and loved every splattered minute. That was twenty years ago, but the family and I have remained close, so much so that for my husband's last two sabbaticals from the University of Saskatchewan—part of each were spent once again in New Zealand—I got to go back to my farm family. They now have sheep and deer several kilometres further up in the hills from the old dairy farm. The last time we went back, I woke up early in the morning, pulled on my Wellingtons and, with the Tammy the fat corgi, climbed up into the hills to the highest point on the farm. After the sheep settled down and were content to simply stare, I sat down.

The vista was incredible: a 360-degree clear morning view of the Matahuru Valley as far as one could see. Almost to the Coromandel Peninsula in one direction, farms spread out in the valley below; if it had been a clear night, the Sky Tower in Auckland would have been a tiny speck of light to the north-west. The ponga trees clung in feathery clumps in the gorges below, and the air was so clear and pristine that I could hear a dog bark and a shepherd calling commands as they worked a flock maybe 5 kilometres away. I sat there, the only person at the top of the world—on the bottom of the world—and quietly soaked it up, drank it in. This was not a moment to be rushed. When I was sated, I called Tammy and began the trek back down into the valley.

Our youngest son is heading off to Europe in a couple of weeks. His first big adventure. We've begged all three of our children to travel, and this is Ben's first time abroad. I tell him my Matahuru Valley story and plead with him to find a grassy hillside in France or Italy or Germany, sit down, be still and quiet, and drink in another part of the world.

> KARIN MELBERG SCHWIER, SASKATOON, SASKATCHEWAN

Last summer, I left my home in Halifax and went to work on a farm for the first time. I was weaned from city life on a crop that hasn't captured the urban imagination: tobacco.

The work was as unromantic as second-hand smoke. Hunched over in a hot, humid greenhouse, I pulled plants from the ground and packed them into green plastic crates, pushing hard on the roots to make room for more. As I filled each crate, I carried it the length of the greenhouse and hoisted it into the truck outside.

After a couple days of cloud and rain, the southern Ontario skies cleared and the temperature in the greenhouses climbed over 30 degrees. Dirt from the roots of the young plants coated my clothes and hair and filled my sneakers. In spite of the sauna-like conditions, my back muscles ached. I started taking aspirins on my juice breaks. And I begged a heating pad from the farmer to use at night. I cursed tobacco. The dirty plant was breaking my body.

Each morning, while I was climbing gingerly out of bed, the farmer was already in the greenhouses. Each evening after supper with his family, he disappeared back into the fields to tend his tobacco. He pulled it, he planted it, he watered it. When he wasn't working with it, he worried about it. The nights were too cold, the days too wet or the sun too hot. Tobacco was on his mind all day, every day.

The miracle is, he found it beautiful. After supper on the day we finished planting, he suggested a ride in the pickup. We stopped to survey each of the fields. The one just planted, its tobacco small and wilted. And the one planted on the first day, the plants grown taller and sturdier during their two weeks in the ground. He admired the tidy rows of green plants in the dark soil.

"Now's the only time they're really pretty," he said. "In six weeks, they'll be six feet tall."

As we circled the last of his fields, he dealt me a share in his satisfaction.

"Every fifth plant is yours," he said, crediting my work in the greenhouse, "think of it that way."

Then he turned the truck onto the road and drove away from the farm. The horse chestnuts were in bloom, the lawns of the houses along the road were green and freshly cut. Their bright flowers threw long shadows.

"It's the same light as in the morning," he told me. His comment reminded me that he's worked his whole life at a time of day I've seen only a couple of dozen times. We bought soft ice cream in a neighbouring town, then stopped the truck at the baseball diamond and watched teenagers warm up for a game. Heading home, we caught a breeze through the truck window and a glimpse of the setting sun. He turned down a road, and we stopped to watch the sky redden over a darkening tobacco field.

"This is my country," he said.

I never thought I'd get teary-eyed over tobacco. But I'd never seen it in the late evening sun through the open window of a red Ford pickup. Or through the eyes of a man who grows it.

> WHITNEY MILLER, TORONTO, ONTARIO

The hay is in the barn. That annual harvest ritual which sings to my soul is finished for another year. Hay is made, just as they say, while the sun shines. And the sun that makes it possible keeps it from being light work. If you have never put up a few hundred bales of hay in a barn loft on a sunny summer day, think of lifting weights while climbing a StairMaster wearing a snowmobile suit—in a sauna. Not what you'd call recreation, but, nonetheless, this is something I love.

The rite of bringing in the hay binds me to the earth. It is an act which fills my every sense. The smell of the freshly shorn field. The back of my neck warmed by the sunshine and scratched by itchy hayseeds clinging to trickles of sweat. The view of the LaHave River from the crest of a hill. The rhythmic, whirring thunk of the tractor and baler steadily producing winter's sustenance for our small herd. And the taste of cold well water passed in a thermos from the cab of a pickup truck.

For me, making hay is a labour of love. I am filled with love for my ten-year-old son, Jeff. Feet spread to maintain balance, he is perched on the bales in the back of the truck with his friend Zack. Jeff and Zack are carefully constructing the load, which will have to hold fast till we get to the barn. This is difficult, demanding and important. No one wants to see broken bales on the road between the field and the barn. This is Jeff's first year building the load. He follows Zack's lead and works harder than I have ever seen him do before. His effort fills me with awe. His lack of complaint adds an extra measure to my respect for him.

I look with love on Jeff's younger brother and sister, both silhouetted against the open sky on top of a pyramid of hay. Too small to heft heavy bales, they sit patiently, lost in their own thoughts and quiet in their contemplation. I know they both love haymaking days. The gathering of friends who are so much a part of this harvest. The sense of belonging that comes with community effort—even when your job is just to pass the water jug. Bringing in the hay brings me ever closer to the man I love, who works with a drive I can only try to match. I follow his pickup back to the barn. Smiling at the sight of his elbow out the window. Knowing, even from this distance, that he is bathed is a poignant musk of dust, sweat and hayseed that captivates me.

As we unload the hay from the trucks into the loft, I look around me. We are two young boys, a grandfather, a doctor, a forestry officer and a middle-aged mother of three. Every brow is gleaming with sweat. Few words are spoken in the syncopated swing of bales from the conveyor to the top layer of the growing pile. No words are needed. I look at Jeff struggling with an especially heavy bale. He catches my eye and grins.

As I stand in the loft at the end of the day, I breathe in the sweet, warm smell of the new hay. It is spring rain. It is summer sun. It is the earthy decay of autumn and the quiet slumber of winter. It is a personal treasure—this rich bounty. And through its very existence, my abiding love for my family, for our friends and for the wonder of creation is once again renewed.

> AMY BENNET, BIG LOTS, NOVA SCOTIA

I can never forget my first summer as a farmhand working down the road on a vegetable farm north of Bradford, Ontario, on Highway 11. My brother, a neighbour and I biked the short path through the back field to work every morning and put our (excess) youthful energy to good use. I was eleven, and the boys were thirteen. We had our fair share of accidents in the years we worked there—sunburns, bites, celery poisoning and stitches for deep cuts—but one particular event stands out in my memory.

We had cut cauliflower all morning, and the boxes were lined up in rows, ready to be loaded onto the wagon. Of course, being the only female out on the field, I was never expected to do the fast and heavy lifting, so my job was to hold the tractor steady at 2 kilometres per hour while the boys threw the boxes on behind me. I didn't know anything about operating heavy machinery, and the only way I was taught to stop the tractor was to push in the clutch. We were always working on flat fields, so this hadn't proved a problem. That morning, as I was putting along making sure not to run over any plants, I suddenly heard shouts from the wagon: "Stop! Stop!"

My brother John had slipped hoisting up a box and was under the wagon. I pushed in the clutch with all my might, but the cauliflower field was on a slope, and the big blue Ford kept on rolling. I didn't know what was going on—I was standing on the pedal that had made the mighty machine stop every other time, but it glided perilously onward while I watched the upper half of my brother trying to writhe out from the path of the heavy wheels. I was going to kill my brother. I froze, standing on the clutch, unable to find a way to stop the beast. I wailed aloud, "I can't stop! I can't stop!"

Something flashed beside me, and the tractor shuddered to a halt. I imagined my brother's mashed body was blocking the wheels. I couldn't look back and wailed, "Did I hit him? Is he dead?"

Silence.

It took a moment before I realized that Roger, our ever-practical neighbour, had run up and slammed his hand on the foot brake. I looked down and saw his hand secured on that odd square pedal I never thought to lay foot on. My brother groaned, and I saw then that the wheel was just touching his shoulder. He had been watching it approach, waiting to be crushed as his sister drove right over him, wondering why the tractor wasn't stopping.

For the millionth time, I want to say "I'm sorry, John, for almost killing you." All three of us laugh over it now—John told the story as Roger's best man at his wedding last year—but the laugh is surely on me, as it should be.

> L.N.

Yesterday, the neighbour's cows got loose again. I clambered into my rubber boots, slapped a beret on my bald head and set out into the fields to chase them home. As I ran through the tall grass, I started projectile vomiting. I'm on my third round of chemotherapy, and this sort of thing happens. My poor dog, who is always thrilled to chase cows, didn't know what to make of her mistress when I turned on her and kicked her for jumping up on me. In the end, I was reduced to shouts and tears, clumping home feeling guilty and ashamed. There is absolutely nothing ennobling about this ordeal.

I was diagnosed with breast cancer in March. Since then, I've undergone three surgeries, and there are more to come. I have open wounds on my breast and belly that need dressing twice a day. I feel trapped in a body that continues to betray me. Each piece of it represents a new problem—phlebitis in my arm from the chemo, pain in all my joints, a constant sore throat, a nauseous metallic taste in my mouth, infections, exhaustion, interrupted sleep and everything smells like rotten fruit.

I know I'm one of the lucky ones. My prognosis is very hopeful, my chemo is only three months long, and I've had lots of support from friends, colleagues and my wonderful family. I have a job to go back to; I live in a country where I get the best medical care, all covered; I have a roof over my head and the freedom to live my life as I choose. I have a wonderful partner, and, at fifty-two, I can look forward to many more years of this amazing life on this beautiful planet. Nobody is stoning me to death for my beliefs. Nobody is bombing my home. I don't need to pick through the garbage dumps of the rich to find food. I have a good education and I feel safe in my small community. Why should I complain?

I watched the events of last week [September 11, 2001] on the television in the chemotherapy room. I must confess that I must be one of a tiny minority of people who were hardly affected by this tragedy. There's something so compellingly immediate about impending pain and nausea that it takes all one's attention.

People around me keep telling me how brave I am. They smile a lot and their eyes go soft. I know they're trying to help, and, believe me, I do appreciate their kind words. But it isn't bravery to face something that you had no choice about. I don't feel brave or noble at all. I feel selfish, I feel angry, I feel constantly disgusted by the many indignities that my body imposes on me. I feel mean-spirited. I'd rather *you* had cancer than me! Nothing about this makes me a better person. All I really want is to go away and come back when it's all over.

And yet something *is* different. There's something I've learned from having cancer while watching the world go crazy around me.

In the last week, many people have expressed feeling a loss of innocence, a loss of security, an end to the illusion of safety. Having cancer also takes away these illusions. None of us is safe. Ever.

For me, now, the chemotherapy room is the most frightening and threatening place I can imagine. Adding pictures of planes flying into high-rise buildings doesn't make it any scarier. Nevertheless those pictures made me sad. I wasn't popular with the nurses when I expressed this sadness—that people could be driven to such extreme actions. Nor when I noted the symbolism of desperate people attacking the ivory towers of wealth. The nurses were shocked, but the other patients around me, hooked up to their ivs pumping poison into their bodies in a crude and sometimes futile attempt to fight the cancer within, all nodded quietly. They understood desperate measures. They also sympathized with the underdog.

No, I'm not excusing the attacks. All life is precious. If there's anything having cancer has taught me, it's exactly that: *all* life is precious. Which is why, as I watch the Bush administration preparing to righteously annihilate the lives of thousands of innocent people in Afghanistan, I want to cry out loud. Have we learned nothing in this past century of war?

There is a cancer in the world body that needs to be excised, the cancer of greed, the cancer of hatred. We can't afford to keep ignoring it. Half the human race is rotting away in poverty, oppression and enforced ignorance, so that the other half can indulge in excessive consumption. It's time to heal the whole body. There will be pain, there will be loss, there will be times of despair and selfish anger and tears. But as my doctors keep saying to me: "Consider the alternative!"

> JUDITH QUINLAN, WISTARIA, BRITISH COLUMBIA

I reached up, the morning air, goosebumps rising on my arms, and formed the crane, then slowly lowered my arms pulling the sunlight that shone in my face down the length of my body. My arms framed a circle over my feet; Moon in Water. I exhaled. Two black crows raced and tumbled overhead, bang on time. The whole flock that invaded Gastown every morning with sunrise called their usual welcome to me. I was as much a part of their routine as they mine.

I began practising Qi Gong on the roof of my building overlooking the harbour and mountains beyond in June of 1998, one month after my second operation. The movements, so awkward and disconnected at first, became fluid with growing strength and familiarity over that long hot summer. I grew flowers to scent my meditations and learned to tell, as I moved and breathed in, which plant was closest at any given moment.

The slow and purposeful activity below on the water, the crows that began as audience and later gave every appearance of participating, the blueness of the sky that summer: all seeped into my skin with the sun and became, in those hours I spent alone on the roof, one long deeply felt exhale that blew the fear, restrictions and debilitations of cancer out of me.

> JACQUI PARKER-SNEDKER, BURNABY, BRITISH COLUMBIA

PART 2

I PLACED MY THUMB
UNDER THE DRILL BIT

It occasionally happens that I'll be in some neutral place or circumstance—a store, say, or a taxi—and the radio will be on and I'll have the unsettling experience of hearing my own voice, pretaped, coming out of the speakers. Nothing makes me feel more vulnerable. It's like waking up and discovering that you've been sleepwalking, naked, down Main Street. Many broadcasters—indeed, many singers—will tell you they can't stand the sound of their own voices. It's an unfortunate affliction, perverse really, but it's one that I know very well. I have also heard from any number of candid listeners over the years who want to lighten their loads by telling me how much my voice and/or manner set them on edge, and I never know quite how to answer these inspired criticisms, because I'm very sharing of their discomfort. Mine is not a voice made for the radio. It's on the thin side, a little nasal, and I have an unfortunate sibilance that early orthodontics might have dealt with. Oh, well. One does the best with what one has.

I can comfort myself, when comfort I require, by remembering that the actual presentation of the Roundup, the bit you hear on the radio, is only a small part of the job. The greater responsibility is organizational and editorial, and one of my tasks is to read and to listen between the lines of the letters and calls that come to us, and to find there a hint or suggestion of how one particular story can be spun into another. In gardening terms, I keep on the lookout for promising volunteers. For example, if we've been receiving stories about, say, excuses for arriving late, and someone submits a story about missing a job interview because they got caught up in a funeral procession, the show's direction might veer off in the direction of funerals and the odd things that happen at them.

While the Roundup often progresses in this organic way, it also happens that our ideas come from within. Every morning, our little squad—typically there are six of us—gets together to talk about the show, take on assignments and consider the lay of the land. These meetings are short and informal, and it's not unusual for them to degenerate—or rather, evolve—into genial gabfests, and it's not at all unusual for a story pitch to emerge from collegial gossiping. Ross Bragg has a particularly good nose for sniffing out the themes and tangents to which our audience will warm, and I'm pretty sure it was he who suggested one morning that we should ask for stories about self-surgery: times when people have taken the knife to themselves rather than seeking the advice of a professional. I was sceptical that anyone would do such a thing. As usual, I was wrong.

The first apartment I inhabited by myself was a cold-water flat next to the Royal Bank, on the northeast corner of Broadway and Granville, above a sewing machine store. It had huge rooms with high ceilings and had been inhabited for years by an old lady who had finally gone to live in a home. The walls were grey with the grime from the oil-burning heater in the living room and the oil-fired range in the kitchen. This range would heat water if it was on—but in summer it made the apartment much too hot, and, to keep it going, you had to go out to the back balcony and pump oil into a can from a hand-cranked pump. So, baths in the claw-footed tub were a cold weather luxury. At other times, sponge baths with water heated on a small electric hot plate were the norm. Lighting the oil units was quite a performance. You turned on the oil flow, waited a minute or two until a small pool of oil was visible, then dropped in a lighted piece of paper. Then you waited until the flame stabilized and regulated the flow according to how much heat was desired. This took a while to figure out. Often, on windy nights, a draft would blow out the flame in the living room heater, and I would awake to a chilly apartment and a pool of oil that had to be mopped up before the heater could be relit.

I was in my mid-twenties and my parents were not keen on this place. But they pitched in and helped me to paint the walls white, the filthy floors grey, and the trim in the bedroom and living room orange and bright blue respectively. My dad replaced the worn and cracked lino on the kitchen counter with salvaged Arborite. The addition of Indian-bedspread drapes made the place home. Soon, the walls were decorated with posters and an old crocheted tablecloth I found in the Sally Ann.

The view from my living room window was the North Shore mountains with Pacific Press in the foreground. To my mind, I was situated at the hub of the city. Steps away from buses in all directions. Kitty corner from the Aristocratic Restaurant, open twenty-four hours a day. A great party place and the perfect apartment to begin my life as a poor but happy member of Vancouver's theatre community. Oh—and the rent? A modest $67.50 per month, which included the oil.

I lived in that apartment from 1970 to '72. During that time, I felt freer than I had ever felt before. I had very little money, hitchhiked everywhere except at night and made some lifelong friends. I got my first cat, shopped for veggies in Chinatown and felt myself becoming interwoven with the fabric of the city. Six months after I moved out into a communal house with some friends, a fire gutted the paint store under the east end of the building. The apartments were condemned and torn down. They were old and outdated, but I mourned them. It was that apartment that freed me of my first broken heart. It was there I learned that I could live alone and be happy.

> JANET BICKFORD, VANCOUVER, BRITISH COLUMBIA

My attic flat on Main Street West in Hamilton, Ontario, was one of my first apartments and my most infamous. It was on the third floor of a faded wooden house only steps away from four lanes of solid one-way traffic hurtling through the very heart of Steeltown.

The first time I viewed the flat, a scrawny, chain-smoking dishwater blonde, who looked about thirty-five going on sixty, answered the door and graciously let me sit at her kitchen table while I waited for the owner to appear. I told her I had just landed a short-term job at the university, but I'd need to find other work by the end of the summer. She said I might be able to find a position at her place of employment, a chicken-processing plant where she worked as a professional plucker.

"But frankly, Honey," she told me, "it's a lousy job. You're always wet and you're always cold."

40

I felt a faint chill, wondering if my English B.A. and the '79 recession would force me into such Dickensian labour. Her name was Jeanie, and her rough stringy hands resembled KFC with the crunchy topping removed. While I waited, she showed me her puff paintings—a kind of embroidery using plastic paint that you squeeze from a bottle. She also showed me a hole in her wall.

"Jimmy punched that in the other night," she told me. "He's got a terrible temper." She also told me that Jimmy had just lost his job. Again. About then, the owner—a chubby Gino Vannelli look-alike—showed up. The only entrance to the apartment was up a rickety wooden stairway which snaked up the side of the house. It was covered with a makeshift wall and roof, but there was no light: you went cautiously up the stairs in darkness, fumbled with the lock and burst into a small, but snug, one-bedroom apartment. I wrote my first-and-last on the spot.

I spent the summer there. Every day, I dressed in a crisp, 100 per cent polyester or crimpolene dress or pantsuit—or one of those other non-breathing space-age '70s fabrics—and stood primly at the bus stop in front of the house. This was in contrast to my fellow housemates, Jeanie the chicken plucker, who headed off with her rubber gloves and boots before dawn, and Jimmy, who, it appeared, had replaced employment with a relationship with a large number of burly, black-jacketed men on Harley-Davidsons. I noted, with some interest, Jimmy walking his dog in the park across the street: this involved tying the poor beast's leash to the handlebars of his motorcycle and driving slowly around the perimeter of the park.

It being a fine summer in Hamilton, the sun beaming cheerily through multicoloured blankets of smog, I walked home from work most evenings, often arriving to a group of Jimmy's friends scratching and drinking on the front porch of the house.

"Hi, Terri," they'd grunt and hand me my mail. They never seemed truly threatening, but I was pleased that my father had installed a deadbolt lock on my door. Not that it really mattered, since a fire escape led directly up to a large window that would have opened with the merest hint of force. When I discovered that Jeanie had packed up her puff paints and left Jimmy, I started sleeping with a steak knife under my pillow. But it wasn't really so bad. OK, there was no shower. OK, the kitchen sink never drained properly, and when Gino Vannelli came to fix it, he pulled about a pound of metal strips, nails and bolts out of the pipes. Why, I wondered, didn't he seem surprised? And then there was the fine layer of black grit that I had to wipe off my windowsill every single morning.

But it was my place. I put up people who were visiting Hamilton. I had little dinner parties. And evenings, I huddled next to my twenty-year-old stereo, dreaming of a bright, non-chicken-plucking future and listening to records like Joni Mitchell's *Court and Spark* and, oddly, the soundtrack from *Funny Girl*. At that point in my life, I found Barbra Streisand belting out "Don't Rain On My Parade" to be highly inspirational.

Toward the end of the summer, I noticed that a surprising quiet had settled over the house. No Jeanie and, now, no Jimmy either. Then, one day, I heard the sounds of ripping, tearing and general destruction on the lower floors. Turns out that Gino Vannelli had sold the house to a demolition company but neglected to evict me. By this time, the research project had ended and I had begun a stint in McMaster's Russian Department, replacing a secretary who was away on jury duty. But my inability to use a Cyrillic-alphabet typewriter was a definite career barrier. Fortunately, I had obtained work selling chocolate death masks at the Art Gallery of Ontario's King Tut exhibit and was just packing for my move to Toronto when the destruction crew showed up at my door, pickaxes and crowbars in hand. How sweet not to have to bother cleaning up before I left the place. I didn't even have to take down the *New Yorker* cartoons I'd taped up on the walls.

My last memory of the place was the demolition boys reading the cartoons and chuckling before they put the boot to the walls. If you're ever in Hamilton, flying along in four lanes of one-way traffic on Main Street West, you might glimpse a frozen-meat shop, across the street from the park at

Locke and Main where Jimmy the biker walked his dog. And that, fittingly enough, sits on the site of my apartment.

> TERRI FAVRO, TORONTO, ONTARIO

Once upon a time, I decided to rent a flat on the second floor of a beautiful old house on Wright Avenue in Toronto. The landlord, an eligible handsome Casanova and a fringe alcoholic, lived in a separate flat on the main floor. We would sometimes exchange greetings on our way in and out of the house, but, for the most part, we shared little else.

One day, the landlord paid me a visit. He was a little tipsy and was looking for a playmate. I declined his invitation and several more over time. He would often boast that his reputation was that of a *pig*.

One day, I was contracted to bartend a very private corporate affair. By 3 AM, the party was over. Before I left, I noticed that one of the main topics of conversation that evening was staring right at me. It was the roasted head of a pig, eyeballs and all, resting on a bed of lettuce that lined a silvery disposable platter. Its cheeks were as rosy as the light bulb that lit up in my head. I felt honoured when my request to take the *guanciale* home was granted. After all, it is considered a delicacy by many peoples around the world. At 4 AM-ish, I placed the rosy-cheeked sacrifice in ritualistic style upon the threshold of my landlord's front door. Some time later, he thanked me profusely, but he never bothered me again . . . and I lived happily ever after.

> EILEEN BALINT, GUELPH, ONTARIO

I find our North American arrogance about space a bit disturbing: huge houses for so few people. In other parts of the world, people are quite happy with three generations under a very tiny roof.

My little tower is about 500 square feet. It's on three levels. My long-range plan is to let someone else enjoy being up high among the trees; I plan to move closer to my brook and the earth. I will live in a 400-square-foot single-level house made of clay, straw and sand: traditional materials that are so adaptable to flow of wall and interior spaces. Built-in furniture and niches will make the home like a turtle shell. I have always wanted to live in a turtle shell ... not from a real turtle, of course!

> RIVER TOMINUK, BRITISH COLUMBIA (NOW IN NOVA SCOTIA)

The year we came back from Gibraltar, my brother came home from the pet shop with what looked like two oddly patterned rocks in a box. However, when each sprouted four scaly legs and a head with shiny black boot-button eyes, their true identity was revealed—tortoises.

As anyone familiar with these reptilian creatures will tell you, examining their undersides will provide a clue as to their gender: a concave shell indicates a male, while a flat surface means a female with more room for carrying eggs around. We had one of each, and so promptly named them Richard and Liz.

Dad set about fencing in the back garden so that they could roam at will; however, this was quickly modified as Mum's sweet peas became the focus of their attention, and the speed of a determined tortoise is quite something to behold. Later in the summer, when the strawberries were ripening, they would emerge from under the protective netting with conspicuously red mouths and a self-satisfied air. Although we never found out how or where, Liz and Richard would rival the skills of Houdini and escape quite regularly. We diligently painted their names and addresses on their shells (in non-leaded paint, of course), and then if a neighbouring child found them, they'd bring them back for a reward—two shillings and sixpence was the going rate in those days!

In their second year with us, Richard began to behave rather strangely. He would quietly stalk after Liz, who more often than not was filling her face with some tasty morsel, and position himself carefully right behind her. Lifting his shell high off the ground, he'd lunge suddenly forward, whisking his head inside just before the resounding impact. Liz, finding herself unexpectedly propelled forward, would withdraw into her shell with a surprised wheeze. Round and round the garden they'd crash—Richard in a frenzy of unrequited passion, while Liz showed nothing but callous disinterest in the whole sordid affair, choosing to retire into her "house" with a loud and disdainful sniff. Poor Richard tried valiantly all summer to involve Liz in his amorous advances, but we figured she was a lot older than he and perhaps was beyond being interested. Or maybe she was just being coy, because late one summer, she disappeared for days on end into the steamy compost heap, and we often wondered if a clutch of eggs had been laid. I guess we'll never know as, disappointingly, no baby tortoises ever made an appearance.

> J.S.

It was my sixth birthday, and I received a small turtle and turtle bowl. The bowl was clear plastic, about 4 inches high and 10 inches across, and in the middle was a small island with a plastic palm tree and a ramp for the turtle to climb up out of the water.

I was delighted with my gift and, for no known reason, called the turtle

Twinkletoes. Twinkletoes lasted about three weeks, then died. I can remember how devastated I was and cried copious tears. I finally stopped crying when my mother suggested we have a funeral for the turtle and gave me a Sunkist raisin box for a coffin to put the dead turtle in. It was a grand funeral, complete with the singing of Sunday school songs and a small funeral bier covered with flower blossoms.

Once I recovered from my grief, I took my next week's allowance and headed for Woolworth's and purchased another turtle. Lacking in originality, I also called this one Twinkletoes. Twinkletoes the Second didn't fare any better and soon succumbed. Again, I put the little body in a Sunkist raisin box and had another funeral. Once more, I purchased another turtle, and, if you see a pattern emerging, you're right.

Twinkletoes the Third also got the raisin box. A small area of our garden was beginning to look like a turtle graveyard, with crosses made of Popsicle sticks marking the graves.

I have no memory of how many turtles I went through or when I tired of turtle funerals, but, in spite of my morbid fascination with turtles, I grew up to be reasonably normal. However, every pet I have had since, and there have been many, has had some kind of ceremony to mark its demise.

> DIANE CREBER, ODESSA, ONTARIO

When I was a very little girl, preschool in fact, I used to spend many happy hours with my father and grandfather in the greenhouse, chatting to whoever would listen to me and even those who would and could not; my dolls and my brothers' pet turtle fell into that category. I used to enjoy helping my dad and granddad transplant the young seedlings, although looking back, they must have wished I didn't enjoy their company as much.

My grandfather used to fashion the discarded grape boxes of the previous fall into seedling flats (this was the mid-1960s, and plastic had yet to make it onto the horticultural scene and change things forever) by covering the openings with slats of wood hammered into place; then he would cut them in half on the table saw, thereby making two seedling flats. Before filling the flats with soil, Granddad would bore holes into the bottom with a hand auger so that the water would drain and the soil would not sour.

I took all of this in and realized that a grape box would make a mighty fine crib for my doll, if not a home for the turtle. At some point, I secreted a grape box away from the watchful eye of my granddad, and, together with Dad's hammer and some discarded nails, I began to fashion a bed for my dolls. Everything was going so well until I hammered my thumb. I recall understanding that, should I cry out with pain as I really wanted to do, I would be banished from all tools forever, no ifs, ands or buts.

I did not scream or cry out. I bore the pain in silence, with only my dolls and brothers' turtle for comfort. The cribs turned out great, and I went on to build other creations undaunted, even though I lost my thumbnail.

> NANCY TURNER GOULD, PRINCE RUPERT, BRITISH COLUMBIA

I was building a shed in my backyard recently when I smacked my left thumb with a 20-ounce framing hammer. The thumbnail turned deep purple, and, on a medical pain scale of 0 to 10, the pain was 8.5 and rising. I strode about the yard, holding my mashed thumb in the air, cursing the inventor of the hammer and the god who would allow such needless and unconscionable pain to exist.

The cursing worked, because after a few minutes, the pain began to subside from 8.5 to 7.5 and finally to 4.5, where it remained for the rest of the day. At bedtime, just as I was ready to tuck myself in and read a few chapters of the *Home Handyman*, I noticed that the pain in my thumb was escalating. By the time I turned out the light and attempted to fall asleep, it had risen to an alarming 9.5 on the medical Richter scale of self-diagnosed pain. I swallowed a handful of acetaminophen with codeine and returned to my bed. But I couldn't sleep. I know it's impossible to have a pain of greater than 10, but I swear this baby had broken through the upper limit and was now gyrating somewhere between 11.5 and 15.

After hours of tossing and turning, I finally phoned the emergency ward at the local hospital and asked if there was a doctor on call. The nurse said there was a doctor on call but my case was considered a non-emergency, and I would have to wait several hours before the doctor could see me.

"A non-emergency? Have you ever smacked your thumb with a 20-ounce framing hammer? Have you ever suffered a pain of 15 on the medical Richter scale?"

"Sir," she said smugly, "there is no such thing as a 15 pain. Ten is the limit. My advice is to take two aspirin and go to bed."

In desperation, I phoned a physician friend who was not happy to be roused at 2 AM. "What am I going to do?" I asked. "This pain is going to kill me."

"Well," he said, "in a case like this, we drill a small hole in the nail to release the pressure of the blood behind the nail which is causing the pain." Then he hung up.

I had a drill press in my workshop with a 1/16-inch bit in the chuck. On my way to the workshop, I grabbed a bottle of vodka to sterilize the drill bit and my thumbnail. I placed my thumb under the drill bit, turned on the press and began to drill a hole in the middle of my purple, palpitating thumbnail. I could see little pieces of nail curl away from the bit as it bored into my thumb. Suddenly, there was a flash of pain that set a new record of 30 on the pain scale. I had drilled through my nail into the quick of the thumb. I snatched my thumb away from the drill press and watched in horror as a thin geyser of blood shot out of the hole, spraying an intricate pattern of red dots on the shop ceiling.

After a while, the geyser became a small fountain, and, finally, a slow dribble of oozing blood. As the geyser subsided, the pain also diminished. I could feel it falling from a 30 to a 15 to an 11.5 and, finally, mercifully, to a 4.5, where it remained for several weeks until my thumbnail fell off.

> DAVID SQUARE, TYNDALL, MANITOBA

I am a full-time farmer and I work with my dad on our fourth-generation family farm. Several months ago, I was doing a simple job, when a large P.T.O. shaft crashed down onto my finger and crushed my fingernail. I knew I had only a few more days with that particular nail. Sure enough, it came off. As I went to throw it away, I thought about everything that that nail had done. I put it into my pocket to think some more. The longer I kept it in my pocket, the more I wanted to keep it with me. Much to my wife's horror, I have kept it with me until, now, with the new fingernail almost in place, I must contemplate whether to say good-bye.

What holds me back from ditching my little friend? I think that perhaps it is a tribute to all the parts and tiny pieces that I lose every day—all the hair, blood, skin and pieces of myself that are washed or rubbed away. I think, perhaps, that however young I am, I fear losing myself slowly, and thus I must keep all of me together, if only this small piece in my pants pocket.

> PAUL BROOKS, MOUNT ALBERT, ONTARIO

I carry a totemic item in my purse—my McMaster University meal card, from 1976. It's a plastic photo ID card that I had to present at the residence cafeteria before being served up a high-starch meal, twice a day, five days a

49

week, by ladies in hygienic white dresses and hairnets. If memory serves, I went vegetarian in 1976 and ate only blocks of cheddar cheese and Jell-O salad twice a day, every day. On weekends, I survived on canned beans, sauerkraut and Blue Nun (a cheap white wine I could buy, at the time, for only five bucks a litre).

But it's not for memories of fine dining that I keep moving this card from purse to briefcase to backpack, from wallet to wallet, for the past (gasp!) twenty-one years. It's that picture of me at twenty years of age. It was taken in early September, and Hamilton must have been enjoying some hot late summer weather, because I'm dressed in one of those it-could-only-be-the-'70s halter tops. I was young. I was, despite (or possibly due to) the cheese and Jell-O diet, quite thin. And the camera caught an expression of idiotic optimism that only a twenty year old could have in those heady days of the late '70s, when every item of clothing was unshrinkably synthetic and could be tossed into the dryer without unpleasant consequences. In fact, you could do most things in the '70s without unpleasant consequences. But I digress.

Why do I carry my twenty-year-old self around with me at forty-one years of age? I guess, quite simply, because it's me when I was young. But in many ways, I don't feel that I've changed much. I still can't cook, a fact that could be the topic of a whole other E-mail. I still, if left to my own devices, survive on cheese, although I go for the low-fat mozzarella variety now. And I'm still idiotically optimistic, until I start considering the fact that twenty-one years from now, I'll be sixty-two years of age.

I guess I carry the ID card to remind myself that I am still, in some ways, what I was at twenty and that, with luck, I'll still be that person twenty years from now. On the other hand, it could be that I looked so damn good in that halter top.

> TERRI FAVRO, TORONTO, ONTARIO

My mum died in 1988. In the last days of her life, as we began the clearing-up process, we discovered over forty business cards from the university in her drawers, in purses, in pockets, etc., stating that she wished to donate her body to medical science, with clear instructions on how we could reach the Department of Anatomy. And so, her body remained at the medical school for four years, and no doubt provided some valuable lessons for students! As is the custom, her body was then cremated by the university, and we were called to pick up her ashes.

Now, my mum was an elegant, gracious, well educated, community force to be reckoned with! You can imagine our surprise at the medical school reception desk to be handed "Grannie," as we referred to her with great love, in a black plastic box in a brown paper grocery bag. The paper bag was labelled "Mrs. Sparling—to be picked up." It struck us as hysterically funny for such an elegant woman.

Her ashes were interred alongside those of my father in the sanctuary wall of the Anglican cathedral where my dad had been the rector. Our son, who was not able to join us for the interment, but who loved (and loves) his grannie a lot, said to us on the phone that day, "Why did you buy an urn instead of using her purse?"

"Her purse?"

"Remember," he said, "how attached she was to it? She took it every-where—to the bathroom, to the dining room. An urn might make her nervous."

And so, with great and affectionate giggles, we began the wondrous story-telling that helps fill the void left by those we love so deeply when they leave us; the stories that begin with: "Hey! Remember when..."

> DARIEL BATEMAN, CALGARY, ALBERTA

On beaches, the secret is to *not* pick up anything. You pick up one shell, one stone, one piece of driftwood, and the next thing you know, your pockets are straining at their seams, your pants are threatening to descend to embarrassing levels, and you end up with yet another pile of treasures to trip over. But...do you have any idea how difficult it is *not* to pick up that first object?

Lake Ontario beaches in Mississauga yield all sorts of fascinating flotsam and jetsam. If you walk there with your dog, you will have, of course, armed yourself beforehand with a large quantity of plastic bags. So there we were one wintry afternoon, bumbling along, snuffling in the breezes. But wait. What was that lavender thing undulating in the shallows? I tried to reach it. Icy wavelets lapped at my shoes. I eyed the dog. Somewhere in her motley parentage is a retriever or two. I pointed. "Get the ball!" I ordered. She wagged her tail and looked at me like I was a nice person, but crazy. I ran higher onto the beach and retrieved a stick. The dog spun her tail in circles, at triple speed. With her enthusiastic support, I poked the stick into the water and dragged out what looked like a length of fabric.

It *was* a length of fabric!

At this point, I should confess that I am a fabric-holic. Whoever wrote the bumper sticker that says "She who dies with the most fabrics wins" must have first peeked into my fabric cabinets. My many fabric cabinets. Here, free for the taking, was a mostly clean, never-been-used metre of lavender broadcloth! Chortling with glee, I wadded it into one of my plastic bags. And what do you think I found a few steps farther on? You guessed it—a metre of yellow! Then the red and green metres floated together, in reach of my stick. When I spotted the black and white metres, also never sewn and merely torn from their bolts, I was, somehow, not surprised. I reeled them in, too.

I began taking the dog for walks on the beach every day! Twice a day! I found more fabrics, some usable (after washing), others not. And then, from the bank above the beach, I spotted something else: something black, with square corners. The dog joyously leading the way, I scrambled down to discover, half-buried in the sand, a sturdy plastic box. Small, but perhaps useful for some as-yet-unplanned project? I clawed it out of the sand. No lid. I dumped the sand out of it. There was a label on the underside of the box. Blinking in the chilly wind, I fumbled for my glasses. "Cremated Remains," I read. The box landed on the beach with a thud. Someone else could take home *that* particular treasure...

> JANET BOLIN, MOUNT VERNON, NEW YORK

When my father passed away, we decided to place his ashes in a Glayva liquor metal container. It seemed fitting. He liked the odd drink and was born in Glasgow, Scotland, which is the native land of Glayva. We also saved over $100 on a fancy container and could drink the bottle at the wake.

We took the ashes to a small cove my parents liked to frequent. It was a blustery December day. I gingerly carried the box over the slippery rocks to the water's edge. The box was extremely heavy. Dad was not a large man. He would have been proud of his weighty ashes.

We said our good-byes, and I pried open the Glayva box, opened the plastic bag that held the remains and prepared to scatter his ashes onto the waves. Just then, a gust of wind raised up a blur of grey ash. There was much coughing and choking. We brushed ourselves off and had a few giggles about Dad's last joke; then, I emptied what remained of the remains into the cold sea.

A coin-size metal object fell from the tin can.

"Look! Dad left some change in his pockets."

"Where is it?"

We searched the shallow water and found what proved to be an identity marker used by the crematorium. Mother noted that any money would have legally been hers, and then it started: not the wrangling over family wills, but the giggles. They lasted most of the day, even into the wake, a good Scottish-Canadian wake. Damn, it felt good. There was lots of time for crying later on.

> STEVE WALKER, KIMBERLEY, BRITISH COLUMBIA

In April 1998, our son, Sean Francis Cyril James, died suddenly at the age of eleven. It is as painful as every parent imagines it would be.

Sean was a joy and had a wonderful sense of humour. His laugh was a mighty, contagious laugh—we miss it. He also loved music. It was wonderful, as a parent, to be able to sneak up behind him when he was busy with his Lego or Plasticine creations and listen to him humming everything from U2 to Handel.

Sean died on a Thursday in Halifax at the IWK hospital. He was surrounded by his family and friends, his doctors, nurses and others. After helping to clean his body and to pack up our belongings, thank the incredible staff and make the necessary phone calls, we went to the ground floor of the IWK to exit. Anyone who has ever been there will know about the machine that you put your parking voucher into. It calculates your cost and demands that you feed it with the appropriate coins. Having done so, it promptly warns you that you only have a matter of so many minutes to exit the parking facility. After fumbling for change—there were three of us leaving at the same time—and thinking that we were all ready to go, I remembered that we still had the key to the room that the staff had provided us with. My daughter, Jessica, and I raced back upstairs, returned the key, thanked everybody again and ran back downstairs.

Everybody who owned a watch in our crowd was standing there wide-eyed, counting the minutes left on our opportunity to escape the parking garage. We went out to our vehicles, which were conveniently parked in close proximity. Threw things into the car. Ran around to share hugs with friends from Nova Scotia and Ontario, and sprang into our seats. You could almost hear some omnipotent Lorne Greene–style voice beginning the count down: 20–19–18–17. It was a scene from the Keystone Kops—luggage flying, hugs, tears, children running from one car to another. Everyone was convinced that we were crazy. I suppose we were, with grief.

On Saturday morning, early, three of our dearest friends and neighbours—Judy-Anne, Nancy and Celia—arrived, food in hand. We started telling stories about our children, our friends and other experiences around death. Before I knew it, we were sitting closer together on the floor, laughing. We looked up, with tears streaming down our cheeks, to see an older woman, who knew our children well, standing in the doorway of the living room with a look of—well, not quite shock, but certainly of puzzlement. It only served to make us laugh harder. I am sure that we must have looked so odd, but I can tell you it was just what I needed that morning.

> SIOBHAN LASKEY, GAGETOWN, NEW BRUNSWICK

Picture two exhausted sisters—we'd just buried our mom six weeks earlier—sitting in the first pew, waiting for the Legion padre to begin the funeral service for our dad. The padre didn't know Dad, but someone had provided him with a card with a few notes about him, and his name. Dad had a nickname, so his first name was recorded as James (Rusty). The padre registered the first bracket as a "C" and called our dad "Crusty."

The first time it was spoken, my sister and I looked at each other in horror. By the tenth utterance of "Crusty," our shoulders were heaving, trying to suppress ourselves from bursting into belly laughs! The tears were pouring down our cheeks, our hands were over our mouths in agony, hoping he would not say "the word" again. Our friends and relatives thought we'd been sobbing our hearts out, hence the heaving histrionics. Shell-shocked, we apologized to Dad later for laughing at his funeral, but knowing Dad, he was probably laughing as well. (He'd been called a lot worse in his lifetime.)

> w.

When I was a child, my dad and I would often visit my great aunts Martha and Maggie on their southwestern Ontario farm north of Dutton. Perhaps it could best be described as the place that time forgot. Back in the early 1960s, the Dutton area was still mainly populated by the descendants of the stalwart Scottish settlers who had cleared the land a hundred years before. Martha and Maggie lived in an old clapboard house, weathered a muted grey. In the backyard, the well and hand pump still provided them with their water.

The back door (I never used the front door—I don't think there were any steps) led into a gigantic farm kitchen. Covering the length of one wall was a still serviceable black wood stove and by the door was the phone—a wooden wall model, operated by a crank! The one concession to modernity was a large white refrigerator, which stuck out incongruously, its proper place never considered when the house was built.

Smack dab in the middle of the room, with enough space to sit a dozen farmhands, was the kitchen table. I believe it was painted white and I'm sure it had one of those plastic red-and-white checked tablecloths. It was generally occupied by my dad's cousin "Dunc," who worked the farm for the aunts. Seated at the table, you could see everything that went on in the room.

Great Aunt Martha spent her time bustling around making tea and home-baked cookies. She was very clever and doted on my father. I was a great disappointment to her because I was the last chance to carry on the family name and turned out to be—horrors—a girl. Aunt Maggie generally reclined on a worn fainting couch in the corner. They both had grey hair braided and wound around their heads. You knew that if you ever saw them in their nightclothes (which, of course, you never would), their hair would, uncoiled, fall to their waists.

Aunt Maggie eventually disappeared from the scene when she was committed to the Ontario Hospital (now called the St. Thomas Psychiatric Hospital). I don't know why. Perhaps someone told her the twentieth century had arrived. Once, when we visited with my mother, we sat in the front parlour. She was apparently considered company. It was very dingy and full of needlepoint. I found myself drawn back to the kitchen with its white wooden walls, linoleum floor and, of course, the gigantic table that dominated the scene. It was definitely another time and place, and one I feel fortunate to have encountered.

> MARIDON DUNCANSON, LONDON, ONTARIO

There were things I should have learned from my four maiden aunts, but I didn't, and things I did learn from them but, perhaps, should not have.

The first thing they said to me when they arrived in the car to take me anywhere was, "Did you remember your hanky, dear?" When it came to boys, their advice could be summed up in one word: "Don't."

And I didn't. For years, I didn't. On my sixteenth birthday, everyone teased, "Sweet sixteen and never been kissed!" And it was true, oh, too, too, heartbreakingly true! I had to go to considerable pains to engineer a first kiss. And then I was eighteen, and going away to school, and I had not yet engineered a second kiss...

I knew all about romance, though, from books. "The Kiss" happened at the end, after about two hundred pages of near misses. We'll call him... Jerry. Jerry knew all about romance, too. Evenings, he met me at my dorm and took me out, never divulging our destination beforehand, for a "study break." We walked. I laughed so hard it hurt. He played his harmonica, a tune he had composed—for me? He held my hand—we must already be past page fifty! In one of the school's deserted lounges, while Johnny Mathis crooned "Smoke Gets in Your Eyes," Jerry whirled me around, transforming me from a gawky schoolgirl wearing a bulky sweater and ski pants to a glamorous woman in a gorgeous, floating gown. Another student came in and plunked down to study. It kind of affected the mood, but it was time for me to leave, anyway. Girls—and glamorous women—weren't allowed out past curfew.

The night of the Big Snow, Jerry stamped my name, JANET, in huge letters on the quadrangle. Could this... possibly... be Love? He called the next night. "Dress warmly," he said. Beside an empty parking lot, he knelt at a plowed-up mountain of snow and announced, "We're building an igloo!" Giddily, I helped scoop out a burrow. Had we already passed page one hundred? Were we heading for "the Kiss"? In our igloo? Before curfew, that very evening? There was just enough space inside for our upper bodies. Leaning back on my elbows, I studied rooftops on the street below us.

I heard Jerry turn his head toward me.

I felt his breath on my cheek.

Across kilometres and years, my maiden aunts' question whispered through my mind like a taunt: "Did you remember your hanky, dear?"

How could I let him kiss me when my nose was running so copiously I could taste it? I couldn't snuffle it back, could I? Or... wipe it on my sleeve? Jerry and I had not yet reached anywhere near two hundred pages of near misses, had we? There would be other chances, wouldn't there?

Wouldn't there...?

On another snowy night a week or so later, I heard a harmonica playing Jerry's tune. In the dorm? Boys weren't allowed in the girls' dorm. I eased my door open and peeked out. There, in the hallway, stood Jerry's new girl.

Her face and fingers rosy, as if she'd just come inside, her eyes ablaze with—triumph? She was playing Jerry's tune.

And staring over her harmonica, right back at me.

> JANET BOLIN, MOUNT VERNON, NEW YORK

I was twelve years old—a country "farm girl," ready to go to high school in Renfrew. One summer, my uncle, who lived in Admaston, hired a boy to help on the farm for the summer. Eddie's mother was anxious to get him away from the big city for the summer. He was fifteen at the time—a well-tanned, muscular, handsome hunk of *male*. This was the first that I had ever even noticed a boy!

We went over to visit my uncle on a Sunday afternoon in our old Model A Ford. I was dressed in my Sunday best—a white piqué homemade dress with blue-and-white gingham trim. My Aunt Audrey suggested Eddie and I go for a walk down the farm lane. It was a very hot day. We sat down by the tree trunk in the shade. Who knows what we talked about? All I remember is that first fatal kiss. His lips were thin—but the kiss was as cherries to a caged bird. Later in the afternoon, on our return, my aunt took our picture outside the barn door. Eddie had his arm across my shoulders—at her suggestion, as I recall.

My life has never been the same. We dated for about three or four years. He became the fastest runner in the local high school—Renfrew Collegiate—and played a mean trumpet! We used to meet in the curtains of the auditorium at noon for a few mad kisses, and we walked up to the Haramis restaurant to eat our bagged lunch with a shared cup of tea served in a china pot. Although our paths separated, *forever* he has been the "love of my life." Every kiss since has really been an enactment of that first kiss.

> JEAN SMITH, OTTAWA, ONTARIO

My four siblings and I were not preacher's kids, or PKS. We were RKS, rabbi's kids. In the 1960s, my parents were transplanted from New York to Winnipeg, where they have lived and worked ever since. Over the years, they have faced numerous challenges, and many of them involved us kids, who had to learn, along with them, how to live on the prairies and how to behave like a good rabbinical family. My mom tells stories of her early days in Winnipeg, spending hours dressing us up in snow gear, only to have to undress and redress us when we inevitably needed to go to the bathroom. Trudging to the Main Street bus, we often required rescuing by her when we sank waist-deep into the snow. Not what a girl from the Bronx is used to!

But it was my father, I recall, who learned the hard way to be patient with us and whose work was most often affected by our behaviour. Over the years, he has had to simultaneously lead worship services and keep us occupied or out of harm's way, or to discipline us from afar, mixing his parental and clerical roles for our benefit. More than once, I recall that in the midst of worship, his stern authoritarian voice could be heard emanating from the pulpit, commanding (or was it pleading?), "Would my son and his friends kindly refrain from talking during services!"

The best memory I have of our years as RKS came early on in our time in Winnipeg. In those heady days of Vatican II, great strides were taken in bettering relations between the Jewish and Catholic communities. In the spirit of this new openness, my parents often invited Catholic clergy to dine with us on the Sabbath. One of the first times that we had such a meal—my brother and I were probably aged two and four at the time—disaster struck. My brother, a rather free spirit, ran into the dining room, holding the sacramental loaf of bread above his head, wearing nothing but a small yarmulke and a big grin! This left my father with embarrassing questions to answer as to the nature of the Sabbath meal: "No, no, it is not usual for children to appear with the ritual objects in a natural state."

Unaware of the flap he had just caused, my younger sibling happily dashed off to enjoy some playtime in another room. About an hour later, when the meal was in full swing, my brother re-entered the room with great fanfare and a less than joyful noise. Screaming out for *abba*—the Hebrew word for "dad"—he announced that he had fallen and hurt himself. As is true in many homes, he was searching desperately for the only available painkiller, a kiss on the wounded area from the healing lips of a parent.

My father, always willing to oblige in such matters, began to ask the tear-soaked toddler where his boo-boo was.

"Is it on your elbow?"

"*No!*"

"On your leg?"

"*No!*"

"So where is it?"

"*I hurt my penis!*"

A look of horror swept over all assembled, especially the nuns who were, I am sure, not accustomed to the use of such words or, worse still, such a request. However, my father—already a well-experienced parent—quietly offered my brother a kiss on the forehead as a remedy to his ailment. Satisfied and recovered, the little nudist went on his way and the meal resumed without incident.

That was, until I became fascinated by the crucifixes hanging around the necks of our guests. Living a very Jewish life, I had no idea what these strange objects were and, without so much as a moment's hesitation, darted over to the first nun I saw and began examining the mysterious item. Shaking it from side to side, I was mystified and a bit upset.

"This thing is no good," I announced. "It doesn't tick!"

This elicited an uproar of laughter and was the beginning of many years of warm friendship between our family and this order of special nuns who did not mind teaching us about their ways or learning themselves about ours.

Years have passed, and my little brother (now clothed on a more or less regular basis) is himself a rabbi. In fact, he is the chief rabbi of Japan and lives in Tokyo. He is also the father of a daughter and will in time, I am sure, face many of the same situations that my poor abba did in Winnipeg.

> AVI ROSE, TORONTO, ONTARIO

This is the strange story of the one and only supposedly scientific experiment in which I have participated. It was about thirty years ago, at the Clarke Institute of Psychiatry in Toronto. I can't remember how the notice described the experiment, but the price was right for a poor student.

I arrived at the appointed hour and was asked to take off my pants and underwear, sit in a large recliner and look at pictures projected on the wall. Affixed to my penis was what looked like an old-fashioned small milk bottle, with a foam neck at one end and a small nozzle at the other, to which was attached an air hose that sucked out the air to create a vacuum. Apparently, this rig, decorously covered by a towel, enabled the experimenters to measure blood flow in relation to the pictures shown, which alternated between pictures of Parliament, the queen and cross-sections of women, knees to waist or waist to neck. I believe they were observing me from behind a two-way mirror.

I did my best not to laugh because I wanted to collect my fee. Due to the vacuum and the towel, I could not gauge my own reaction, if indeed there had been any. Following this test, I answered a battery of questions about what sorts of sexual acts I would engage in, many of them entirely unknown to me as a first-year university student. I never did find out the results, but my first brush with experimental psychology was enough to make it my last.

> PATRICK COTTER, VANCOUVER, BRITISH COLUMBIA

PART 3

THE MOUNTIE LOOKS
VERY RELAXED

I often feel an irrational surge of something like pride when a letter or call begins with the phrase, "I never thought I would write to you, but this time, I couldn't resist." Typically, these correspondents are rising to the bait cast by listeners/writers whose particular and unique experience—the night they raided the orchard, the time the dog got skunked and rolled on the wedding dress, the day the baby went for a ride in a dumb waiter—has struck a chord with a complete stranger, possibly thousands of miles away. Those sympathetic vibrations have shaken loose or wakened a memory, dormant who knows how long, of an event or happenstance in his or her own life, and now it needs to be told. In this way, two people, who will probably never meet, forge a union, of a kind, and a small lesson is taught, or reinforced, about the shared nature of experience. And if I feel a pulse of pride, it's because I think the Roundup is doing its job when the airwaves become a wall onto which people can spray their own messages and respond to the musings of those who have passed that way before.

In at least one case, this "call and response" aspect of the show has had a dimensional spinoff. Janet Bickford, from Vancouver, and Janet Bolin, from Mount Vernon, New York, got in touch with each other after hearing one another's letters read on the Roundup, and have become fast friends. Several of their letters have been included in this collection—and many more might have been; if their private correspondence is anything like the wise, witty, and sometimes wistful letters they have sent to the program, then those envelopes would be well worth the steaming.

My Connemara pony, Rascal, had been gelded after three and a half years of leading a life of lust and leisure, and had just graduated from basic training, a young horse still full of beans. He had been put into my care to keep him fit during the winter and spring until his fair-weather owner reclaimed him. After Rascal had enjoyed the run of the pastures for four months, the owner asked me to board him at a riding school to take advantage of their ring and jumps in preparation for the spring shows.

Rascal was not at all impressed by the indoor facilities and the luxurious rubber floors. My usually placid little fellow became an unruly black monster, dragging me through the sawdust at the end of the lunge line, bucking like a maniac when I got on and dancing sideways around the ring like some sort of Lippizaner on acid.

The day of the first show loomed closer. He had calmed down somewhat, but I was still quite apprehensive. I was in the land of push-button ponies ridden by well-heeled little debutantes in thousand-dollar boots. Rascal and I were simply not in this league, no matter what his bloodline read.

The day of the show dawned clear and sunny. His mane braided, his hooves polished, Rascal's ebony coat shone in the sun and he looked incredibly handsome. Our class was called, and we entered the ring. The judge, a woman in a lovely peach suit and gauzy hat, stood in the centre. Rascal seemed calm enough, though I was surprised that at a walk he was passing the 16-hand thoroughbreds. The command to trot came, and we more or less kept it together. He bucked two or three times, but just little ones, and I thought the judge's back was turned. Then, his gait picked up a little, and he began to be rather jet-propelled around the ring. Literally. The change in diet from pasture to stall had given him a lot of ammo in the "wind" department, and, with each stride, he let out a resounding fart.

Usually, this is just a normal part of horse life, but in this surreal setting, with all those proper young women with deadly serious expressions, it just plain struck me funny. The only sounds were the swish of hooves through sawdust and the subtle jingle of bits and bridles, all punctuated with the backfires from my horse.

With each blast from Rascal, I would echo with a snort of laughter. The judge gave us the evil eye from under her hat and that just made it worse. At the command to canter, all hell broke loose. Rascal gave a tremendous buck, complete with sound effects, and made a diagonal beeline across the centre of the ring. Unfortunately, the judge was looking the other way and only turned in time to see us barrelling down on her. Her clipboard went in one direction, her lovely hat in the other, and, incredibly, her shoes stayed just where they were in the sawdust as she leapt out of our way.

Within seconds, we heard our number being called over the speaker: "Would Number 15 please excuse her horse from the ring. Number 15, please exit the ring."

We did exit the ring and galloped happily home, leaving the show ring bereft of the riff-raff that was us.

> SHEILA BOWMAN, NANAIMO, BRITISH COLUMBIA

I remember, when I was a child, my father reading this story from a veterinary medical journal. A veterinarian was called to a farm to examine a cow that had not been eating. The cow was in a barn, hiding from the summer heat. She was visibly bloated and it did not take long for the vet to realize she was not passing gas. Like any good vet, he inserted a surgical tube through the cow's rectum, and, sure enough, gas began to pass.

The procedure took a little time, and, in his boredom, the vet became curious. He had heard that flatulence was flammable, but he had never known for sure, so he lit a match and set it to the end of the tube. The hose became a flame-thrower, quickly setting fire to the hay in the barn. The vet and the farmer managed to escape without injury, but the barn was burned to the ground and the cow did not survive.

> MARK BUSSANICH, VANCOUVER, BRITISH COLUMBIA

Nobody taught me to make electric porridge. I invented it all myself! It was done out of sheer necessity on an Easter camping trip to the mountains of West Virginia, where our 4000-foot campsite reached minus 17 degrees at night. This is the only way to get going when you crawl out of your tent under such conditions, and it kept our group alive—and happy!

Mix up a stiff solid porridge—really stiff, it's going to be diluted. Stir in a large slug of whipping cream and lots of dark brown sugar. Pour in as much bourbon whiskey as you want and then add a slug more. Eat as much as you can, and then a bit more. Crawl back into your tent and maybe wait for summer. The richness of the cream and sugar and the fumes of the now hot bourbon rising into your nostrils is something to experience, especially on a freezing cold morning in the snow. And the Scots think they know all there is to know about porridge ...

The name "electric porridge"? It is said that back in the Depression, denizens of the Glasgow slums used to get a bit of rubber tube, put one end on the gas outlet and the other into a pint of milk. The gas was then bubbled through the milk until it became suitably toxic and ready for the party. A couple of pints of this electric milk apparently took some of the rough edges off life, Ye Olde Tyme equivalent of glue or gasoline sniffing and just as dangerous. Do not do this at home, children.

> ANDY FORESTER, TORONTO, ONTARIO

When we were kids in the late 1960s, we would get a bowl of our mom's breakfast soup before heading off to school. The soup was always started the night before and consisted of a whole chicken in water, flavoured with salt, pepper and slices of fresh ginger. This was brought to a boil and the foam was skimmed off. Then three or four fresh whole abalone were added to the pot and simmered for two hours or so before the stove was turned off for the night.

The next morning, the abalone were taken out, sliced and put back into the pot, and the soup was brought to a boil again. Then, just before serving, my mother opened a bottle of Johnny Walker Red and poured a generous portion into the pot. It was the most delicious soup we ever had and made our day at school very mellow as well.

> EUNICE LAM, NANAIMO, BRITISH COLUMBIA

When I was a child in Prince Edward Island many years ago, and I mean many years ago, our house on Richmond Street in Charlottetown, like many others, was heated by a coke furnace that circulated hot water through ornate cast-iron radiators in every room. Pans of water would be put on top of the radiators to humidify the house. They were used to dry wet gloves and scarves, too.

One cold evening, just before Christmas, my father took a large piece of beef and enclosed it in a kind of wire basket with long handles. He went down to the cellar, which was piled high with coke, opened the furnace door and plunged the meat inside, holding it over the white-hot coals. Occasionally, he would take it out, look at it, turn it over and plunge it back into the inferno raging inside. It was kind of scary!

After a while, he clanged the furnace door shut, brought the meat back upstairs and served it to us, along with the vegetables prepared by our mother, with P.E.I. potatoes leading the list. There were five children then. Three of us are left now.

He told us that he had broiled the meat. I don't think the word "barbecue" was in use at that time. Perhaps it didn't even exist! (This was before the war, probably about 1938 or so.) In any case, that meat was the best I ever tasted. He never did it again, and I forgot about it until many years later when I barbecued my first steak over charcoal. Suddenly, the memory of that delicious meat was rekindled. It still makes me salivate. No barbecued steak has ever quite captured the flavour of that meat broiled in the furnace. I wonder where the wire basket went?

> FRED COYLE, VICTORIA, BRITISH COLUMBIA

When I was growing up, there was always an abundance of home baking at our house; the kitchen counter groaned under pies, cookies, cakes, muffins and homemade bread. My mother took pride in feeding everyone and everything that came in the door, from kids to kittens. I'm sure it was one of the things that my best friend during my teen years liked most about my house, and one of the reasons we spent a lot of time hanging out at my place.

Then came the day when my friend decided he was getting a little too portly. He set a strict diet for himself and started refusing even my mother's homemade goodies. Worried that he was taking things too far, my mother became more and more insistent that he "have a snack" whenever he dropped in, tempting him with every treat that issued, mouth-wateringly steamy, from the oven. Filled with the resolve to be thin, he wouldn't give in. Neither would my mother. It became a battle of wills.

He arrived at the house one day just after a batch of golden-crusted bread had been set on the counter to cool, and, of course, my mother offered him some. He refused with his usual politeness. She doggedly cut a thick slice for him anyway and daubed it with butter. How could he resist? She held it out to him; he wouldn't take it. She waved it under his nose, steaming and dripping butter and smelling like a baker's dream. His resolve wavered for an instant, but then, unbelievably, he laughed and turned away.

That was it for my mother. In the next breath, she was chasing him around the kitchen with the slice of bread held high, determined to cram at least one bite into his mouth. He ducked and wove and bumped into the table and tripped over the chairs in a futile attempt to escape, but it was no good. He finally collapsed against the cupboards, laughing too hard to run any more, and my mother triumphantly stuffed the bread into him. He ate it then with good grace, and I don't think he refused many of her food offerings after that. It just wasn't worth the potential consequences.

> SHERRY D. RAMSEY, SYDNEY MINES, NOVA SCOTIA

M y father lived the last two years of his life in an extended-care hospital. My four sisters and four brothers and I knew how much he hated it there, and on our regular visits, we tried to bring him things we thought would make life a little more tolerable. Food was an obvious choice because the intense flavours he enjoyed—the sharp tang of pickles and old cheese, Mom's fresh homemade bread, salty baked beans with molasses and bacon, strong dark coffee—did not show up on the hospital menu.

An enthusiastic eater all his life, Dad's robust appetite waned dramatically when he entered the hospital. We tried to rekindle it by stocking the hospital fridge with jars of pickles and asking the staff to be sure to include some on each of his meal trays. On our visits to him, we sabotaged the healthy hospital diet with bags of Cheezies, cans of root beer, and treats of licorice allsorts and chocolate for his sweet tooth.

For a while, this worked. If there were pickles on Dad's plate, he could be encouraged to eat. But there came a time when even that failed. During one mealtime visit, Dad appeared totally disinterested in the blandness on his plate. I tried coaxing and teasing, but he kept his mouth resolutely closed, even when I put a piece of pickle on the fork with the meat. However, when I held out one of the big, green, spicy Sicilian olives I had brought for him, he leaned forward and opened his mouth. Keeping his eyes steady on my face, he chewed it slowly and carefully, savouring every juicy morsel. And he followed that by eating two more! His caretakers told me that those olives were the only food he had eaten in two days.

Of course, he grew weaker; the odd bits of pickle and chocolate we could pop into his mouth were not enough to sustain him. He passed away last March, and I miss him very much. But he is never far from my heart or my thoughts. I think of him whenever I eat a pickle.

> REBECCA PALMER, EDMONTON, ALBERTA

The tool in our house that I would not want to be without is a pickle fork. It is about 8 inches long, with two sharp 1-inch tines on one end and a small plastic pink bumpy knob on the other. It is seldom used for pickles. It is, however, the perfect tool to retrieve objects that have fallen into a drain, to poke holes in leather belts or the top of plastic bug jars, to test the doneness of baked potatoes, to steady something so that it can be cut with a knife, to extract lint from the corners of shirt pockets or from between where the button is sewn on and the edge of the shirt front; it's also a screwdriver, a toy sword, a map pointer, a back-scratcher, a frozen orange juice lid–lifter, a shoelace knot–loosener and a scraper-offer of kitchen goo. Hardly a day goes by that it isn't the perfect solution for something. And every time someone uses it, we remark what an indispensable little tool it is.

> WENDY STEVENS, BROOKLIN, ONTARIO

I took a new friend from England to the local photo shop in my little boat. We could have walked, but it's a long way on foot. Waves were high by the time we approached the beach nearest the store, so we surfed ashore to conduct our business. Back to shore, back into the boat, but the waves were now over 4 feet high.

We managed to launch the boat despite the surf and were headed for home, but it was a warm, sunny day, and so we decided to cruise to the nearest island to check the beaches there for nice shells. We had a good time and made some interesting finds, but as we tried to leave, a 6-foot curler flipped the boat over on top of us on the beach. We came through fine, but my outboard *and* my new camera were both drowned in salt water. It was a long row home.

The outboard was easy enough to preserve for later repair: just open up everything that would open and flush it with fresh water, then methanol, then gasoline, then a thin coat of motor oil. It's since been repaired and runs just fine. The camera was a different story...

I phoned the store where I'd purchased the camera, and they told me that the best thing was to thoroughly flush everything with lukewarm water (to remove any grit that might be in there) then pack it in fresh water until I could send it to Pentax's California service depot. I've been fairly impoverished since then, and the camera has still yet to be serviced, so I still keep a zoom lens in a 1-litre Mason jar and a camera body in a larger peanut-butter jar.

I give them both a scrub with a toothbrush now and then and refresh the water they're packed in to slow algae growth, but there they sit to this day: Pentax pickles... preserved until the money is available to service them.
> MICHAEL MUIRHEAD, QUEEN CHARLOTTE CITY, BRITISH COLUMBIA

In the photograph, I'm standing next to a Mountie. I'm about ten and a half, and my head comes up to the button on the flap of his breast pocket. We're standing in front of the Parliament buildings in Ottawa. It's a hot sunny day. I'm smiling a smile that is really me squinting in the sun, as I am in most of the photos ever taken of me out of doors. My teeth show. I'm probably wishing Dad would hurry up and take the shot before I have to shut my eyes against the glare.

The Mountie looks very relaxed. He stands at ease with a wide but closed-mouth smile. His eyes are shaded by his hat. I'm wearing a dress made for me by my mother. She used to make all my dresses, though we called them frocks then. I remember her making this dress in particular.

The photo is slightly out of focus. The fabric of the dress is a very pale turquoise organdy, with lots of tiny turquoise and pink flowers on it. The skirt is cut out of a full circle so I could spin around and it would swirl out around my legs. It has a full circle of lining material, a sort of self-slip, under it. The front of the bodice is made with narrow vertical tucks in it to give the almost sheer fabric a more opaque look. The round neck has a little gathered frill of doubled-over fabric, and the cap sleeves are gathered, too. There is a narrow velvet ribbon belt of darker turquoise which ties at the back in a bow, and the finishing touch is a flower on the bodice, made from the fabric, tied with a smaller velvet ribbon bow whose tails hung halfway down to the waist.

I remember being very excited as she was making the dress. It was for my first birthday party in Canada, doubly special because it was my first decade. So it was a party dress. At my sister's birthday party, all the little girls were wearing confections of nylon and lace. Dorothy is younger than I, but her birthday comes before mine, so she had a Canadian birthday party before I did. That was when we discovered that the dainty little sandwiches, the lovely cakes, the meringues and eclairs my mother made so expertly, were not the thing to serve for Canadian birthday parties. The kids wanted hot dogs. For my birthday party, we had hot dogs and Jell-O and a birthday cake, of course.

I remember opening our front door, being the hostess, the birthday girl, as my guests trooped in with their little gifts. They were wearing jeans and plaid woollen slacks with twin-sets. Only one other girl was wearing a dress, and it had come from a store. At some point during the party, I remember the girl in the dress coming up to me with a look of sympathy. "I guess your mother made that dress, eh?" she said.

In retrospect, I don't think the girl was being catty. I think she felt out of place too and wanted to commiserate. Possibly her mother had made her wear a dress to the party. Probably I was so desperate to fit in, and there was so much I didn't know about our new country, that I felt snubbed by her remark. I'm wearing it as a summer dress in the photo because it won't fit me much longer and my mother thinks I should get some wear out of it.

What I haven't told you is that my sister is standing on the other side of the Mountie, wearing a dress of peach-coloured lace, also made by my mother. One day, I don't know why, I cut her out of the picture. I could invent a reason why, but I really can't remember what was going through my mind when I did it. Nor do I remember whether I threw out the part I cut off or whether I just lost it. One of life's little mysteries.

> JANET BICKFORD, VANCOUVER, BRITISH COLUMBIA

About twenty-three years ago, I was a young boy growing up in the east end of Hamilton. Every Saturday morning, while my mother was at work, my dad would pack my sister and me into his 1971 Volkswagen Beetle and take us to visit my grandparents, who lived on Hamilton's "mountain." My dad would barely have the car stopped when I would leap from the car into my grandfather's garage and head out on my bike to cruise the neighbourhood. Imagine my dismay when one morning I arrived to discover my bike had been stolen from the unlocked garage overnight.

This was not "just" a bike. Huge chopper handlebars, a lime-green metallic banana seat complete with sissy bar and an orange Fibreglas pole with a triangular flag on top that I had ordered from a Cheerio's box. It was speed incarnate, cool on wheels, and a wheelie waiting to happen. I made a sad round of the neighbours, asking if they had seen my bike, but to no avail. We reported the heinous crime to the Hamilton police, who assured me they would get right on the caper.

Now, as luck would have it—yes, I do mean luck—the very night my bike had been stolen, my grandparents' hot water heater packed it in and the basement was awash. In an effort to make up for the loss, my dad and grandfather took me out with them to Sears to pick up a new hot water tank. The Sears store was at the opposite end of town, and so off we went. As we walked into the store, my grandfather exclaimed, "Hey! Isn't that your bike?"

There it was, leaning against a fence in the garden centre of Sears, at the Centre Mall, beside a 20-pound bag of sheep manure. We were now in a perfect position to catch these bandits and ensure justice was done. Sure enough, two rather Dickensian-looking toughs exited the store and walked toward the bike. My dad and the store manager approached the youths and spoke with them. One of the lads said that he had already had enough trouble with the cops and beat it; the second one hopped on another bike (no doubt hotter than a two-dollar pistol) and also scrammed.

Some twenty or so years later, I find myself a member of the Royal Canadian Mounted Police, often responding to bike theft complaints. I usually try to console the young victims with a well meaning, "There, there, now, you never know, your bike just might turn up ... by the way, how's your water heater?"

> CST. STEVE RICHARDSON, ROYAL CANADIAN MOUNTED POLICE

My dad was an RCMP detachment commander in Maple Creek, Saskatchewan, in the mid-1950s. Our basement contained a metal cage that was the jail for the town. My mother would do her laundry just adjacent to this cell, and I used to stay with her and sometimes talk to the prisoners. Mom tells me I would climb up on the bars and tell them that they had been "a bad boy."

What a surreal experience for some drunk to wake up with a hangover, maybe not even remembering being arrested, and having to put up with some kid hanging on the bars berating him.

> ED ANDERSON, WESTBANK, BRITISH COLUMBIA

I was an RCMP kid, and from birth to age eighteen, I lived in nine different houses in several different towns. Each place had its share of stories, but this one takes the cake.

When I was in grade four or five, I decided I was old enough to make my room in the basement of the RCMP station/living quarters instead of being up on the main floor of the house. I set up my dresser and bed and had a cosy little nest to say the least. I also had a cosy cat who slept on my bed.

One particular night, I thought I was having a dream about witches. I could hear them right in my ear, howling, moaning and making the most horrible sounds one could imagine. The sounds would fade away and then come back louder than before right in my ear. I made myself wake up, and, to my horror, I realized that the sounds were not in my dream. Rather, they were coming from the middle of the basement, which happened to be at the end of my bed. I turned on my light and saw my beloved cat facing off with the neighbour's cat.

I called for my dad, who came with his pellet gun, which he planned to use to frighten the two cats into their respective corners. By this time, there were globs of red and black cat hair flying all over the basement. I was hysterical, clutching the covers over my head. "POP" went the pellet gun, immediately followed by a whining squelch and then silence. My cat ran like a shot under my bed. I peered out from under my covers, and there stood my dad, pellet gun in hand, looking at the intruding cat, now deceased.

To this day, I don't know if the neighbour found out that my dad actually shot their cat, but I do know that I soon moved back upstairs in the house. My basement days were over until we moved again and I was a bit more grown up and into loud music, smoking and posters of rock 'n' roll stars all over the wall. That's another story.

> HEATHER FERRIS, VANDERHOOF, BRITISH COLUMBIA.

Twenty-five years ago, as enthusiastic but extremely *naïve* new parents, we decided that if our children ever questioned where babies came from, we would give them the straight facts: no silly euphemisms for body parts, just procreation plain and simple. Sometime later, we learned how wrong we were when our five year old popped the question at the breakfast table.

"Ask your father," I said, rising to make more toast. My husband bravely began—first with the male sexual organs and their functions. Our son's expression started to turn from curiosity to distaste, but his father soldiered on. Switching to the female sexual organs and their "accepted" names, you could begin to see distaste turn to horror until, suddenly, the young student's face lit up. It had all become clear to him. He had obviously misunderstood this whole sordid business. Beaming with joy, he shot up his hand, as if in class, and said: "That's where the Mounties train!!"

In our house, though, we still think of Regina as the Honeymoon Capital of Canada.

> PENNY BAUGHEN, WINFIELD, BRITISH COLUMBIA

In 1959, our family was on a holiday to Regina, Saskatchewan. We were touring the RCMP Museum, when my son Dennis lost his first tooth. He wanted to have it very much. We looked and looked, and then a Mountie asked what we were looking for. We told him our son Dennis had just lost his first tooth and we were trying to find it.

The Mountie got down on his hands and knees and looked for it and found it. The Mountie always gets his tooth.

> SHIRLEY BARROW, TRAIL, BRITISH COLUMBIA

When I was in grade three, our class did an experiment with cola. The idea was that we would take a tooth, set it in a jar of cola and see how long it would take to decay. Once the plan was hatched, all that was necessary was to sit back and wait for a tooth. This was an opportune time for such an experiment. The smiles of my entire class attested to that. The gaping smiles of twenty-eight or so kids meant a short wait.

I was a little more eager than most. A wiggly tooth in my own mouth meant a chance to impress the teacher. The whole class would be focussed on my tooth. Sort of like my fifteen minutes of fame, only stretched out over weeks.

As I dreamed of what a wonderful opportunity this would be. I came up with a plan. I would simply ask to go to the washroom, wiggle my own tooth free and return a hero.

Up went my hand. Permission granted, I headed down the stairs to the washrooms. The place was empty. The way was clear to begin my path to fame. Funny how loose a tooth can seem, until you try to pull it out. I hadn't anticipated any real pain, but pain there was. I turned and pulled it every which way. And finally...out it popped. Eureka!

But my excitement was short-lived. In one sudden move, the tooth slipped from my fingers, and I watched in horror as it slid down the drain of the sink. It was gone, and so was my opportunity. It would be weeks before I would have another loose tooth. The teacher could have ten other teeth by then. I made my way back to class and never told a soul about my botched plan. I can still see that jar on the window ledge and recall the day my grade three teacher announced the experiment.

Eventually, a legitimate fallen tooth was added to the jar. The kid was a hero and hadn't even suffered a bit. As for the tooth, it decayed away in a matter of days.

> CHRISTIENE WHITE-HARPER, LONDON, ONTARIO.

In the fall of 1995, I was a field assistant on a polar bear survey. We were surveying the northeast coast of Baffin Island by helicopter and attempting, through a tagging program, to determine how many bears there were in a particular range. We would spot the bears by helicopter, then the biologist would dart the bear, and we would quickly set to work to put tags in the bear's ears, clip small fur and nail samples, take measurements, then put a tattoo inside the lip of the bear. The biologist had worked with thousands of polar bears and was adept at handling them.

One day, we spotted a family group: a mother and two cubs born that year. The mother was darted first, then the two cubs, and we waited for the drugs to take effect. The biologist would usually test the bears for responsiveness by approaching the drugged bears with his metal clipboard in his hand to see if the bear could grasp it with its teeth. The bears were always awake while we were with them, but their muscles were relaxed because of the drug, so they could only watch us and grunt. Though I often found the experience unnerving, the biologist knew what he was doing. He'd been doing this work for over fifteen years, and his safety record was pretty impressive.

For some reason, on this day, the biologist put his index finger too close to one of the young bear cub's teeth, and one of those sharp canines penetrated the tip of his finger. Because he worked without gloves, his hands were always stained with green tattoo ink.

Sam, the other field assistant and I, once we knew that it was just a little puncture, gleefully hoped the green tattoo ink would stain the little hole in his finger. We thought there was a kind of poetic justice to the thought of his being at the receiving end of a tattoo from a bear, after the reverse being true for so long. We watched the healing progress of that little puncture to see if a green dot would remain, but, alas, the little hole healed up clean. Oh well.

> LYNN PEPLINSKI, IQALUIT, NUNAVUT

In 1986, I had just graduated from the U of A in Edmonton with a degree in zoology and found myself working as a zookeeper at West Edmonton Mall. Back in the '80s, the mall had a large collection of exotic animals. Over time, I got fairly comfortable going in with the young lions and tigers. On one occasion, I was sitting on a 200-pound lion cub, playing with his ears, rolling his head and mock roaring. I was such a professional!

A member of the ever-inquisitive public tapped on the glass to ask a question. Of course, in a situation like this, I was only reading lips, and I stood up to decipher what was being asked of me. Marshall, the young lion, was apparently not finished playing. He jumped up, put his paws on my shoulders and snagged a claw on my upper lip. I tentatively placed my fingers to my mouth and found a substantial wound that was just starting to bleed. Though I had felt confident with these animals, I doubted the wisdom of remaining in the display with these meat eaters with a stream of blood running down my chin. I quickly covered my wound from the public and got the heck out of there.

I visited a walk-in clinic just a few doors down in the shopping centre and had my upper lip sutured. I was mortified that I would have a 2-inch scar extending from the edge of my nose down into my upper lip. For a few months, I had a moustache, but I never really liked it, and now proudly show off my scar. I forget it is there but always enjoy telling the story.

I still work in the field of zookeeping, and many of my co-workers have scars from animals—it would be difficult to find one who doesn't. We often joke about putting a large cardboard cut-out of a zookeeper's body form on the wall in our lunchroom and have everyone draw their scars and label them with the injuring species. I have had to extract the talons of a great horned owl out of the breast of a female co-worker and seen another calmly wait for a python to release his grip so not to make the wound worse.

> GARTH IRVINE, CALGARY, ALBERTA

In my early twenties, I worked in the Wasaga Beach Zoological Park, a public zoo complete with the who's who of the animal world, including elephants. My work included both input and output chores (feeding various creatures and cleaning up after them).

One of the elephants I cared for was a handsome young fellow named Speedy. I was a well-travelled young man of the era and, having seen elephant hair bracelets in India, decided to weave one for me, using Speedy's sparse and wirelike hair.

When alone with him in the elephant house, I fed and patted him, then grasped a single hair in my fist and yanked. Out it came, and poor Speedy leapt and pranced away in his discomfort. Over a period of days, I managed to get enough hairs for a bracelet before Speedy avoided my touch entirely.

Many weeks later, I was passing through the elephant house, having just shovelled out many hundreds of pounds of "shredded wheat," as we called it, when I was suddenly struck fiercely from behind, and rather low, too. The blow was hard enough to lift me off the ground and to leave me with bruised buttocks for a week. I stood up stiffly and turned to see Speedy prancing around his pen, making what could only be described as "elephant snickers."

> GARY OCKENDEN, NELSON, BRITISH COLUMBIA

The University of Manitoba Entomology Department had received a call from someone who had discovered a small tarantula resting on a bunch of bananas in the produce section of a local grocery store. Initially, the shopper thought the tarantula was simply a brown spot, but then, as the bananas were moved, the spot stretched its legs and tried to escape! The produce manager captured the spider in a jar and the Entomology Department was called: were we interested in this specimen?

I have always had a keen interest in insects as well as arachnids and so was dispatched to obtain "the prize"—a tarantula about the size of a toonie.

Back at the entomology lab, we housed our new guest in a terrarium. Now, the problem arose of what and how would we feed it? We placed grasshoppers and baby mice into the spider's new lair but neither proved to be of interest. It occurred to us that the tarantula might be dehydrated after its long journey hidden among the banana bunches, so I placed a Petri dish of water in the terrarium and watched as the tarantula approached the dish, lifted a foreleg and "tested" the contents. The tarantula then climbed into the water-filled dish and lowered its body into the water. I could almost hear an "aahhhhhh" as it soaked itself.

Thus rehydrated, we hoped the tarantula was ready to eat. One of the entomology professors kept a culture of large German cockroaches, which we thought might serve as a possible food source. Into the terrarium I placed a nice specimen bearing long threadlike antennae. The cockroach explored its new domain, antennae waving.

I watched as the cockroach approached the tarantula from the rear. One of the cockroach's antennae brushed the hairs on one of the spider's back legs. In a flash, the spider turned and grabbed the cockroach. Lunch had been served.

The tarantula lived in its terrarium for approximately a year and grew from the size of a toonie to the size of a saucer.

> HEATHER MACIOROWSKI, CALGARY, ALBERTA

A memorable sleepover occurred not within four bedroom walls on a designer mattress but in a high mountain cirque perched on the Alberta–British Columbia border. I had hiked into this secret hideaway before, an arduous 8 miles in from the gravel road, then up and over a steep limestone headwall, behind which lay an icy jewel of lake cradled in scrapes of flowering alpine meadows. Bringing nothing but a fishing rod, a sleeping bag, a foamy and a sheet of plastic, I would lie under a spread of crisp stars and feel myself drifting slowly with the surrounding mountains in the vastness of the universe. Ahhh, the pleasure of cold, clean air sieving through the lungs as you sail into sleep, coyotes yip-yapping in the valleys below.

This occasion, however, was not so idyllic. As I crested the headwall on the way in, I was met with waves of horizontal spray pelting into my eyes. The small lake was whistling and spitting gusts that swept in from the B.C. side. With daylight already diminishing and no choice but to find the best shelter available, I quickly made for a clump of twisted willows whose roots, I discovered, mostly knuckled over the ground rather than through it, because soil was largely absent. This clump was, to be sure, the only vegetation here taller than golf-course turf and could offer at least a minimal windbreak. I did my best to settle in among the rocks and roots, eventually managing to wrap both myself and my bedroll in a plastic cocoon.

I think I listened to the wind for a while. It was not until perhaps 2 AM that I learned I was in fact having a sleepover. At this time, the resident packrat—having both discovered my unannounced intrusion and, no doubt, already scouted out my entire person from toe to head—decided to abandon caution and seize the opportunity. A sudden sharp tugging at my scalp jolted me from a moment of slumber. I sat upright. I swear the cloud cover was so thick I was incapable of seeing even my own hand in front of my face, let alone the rest of the universe.

I should explain that my father was bald at an early age, except, that is, for a fluff of hair on each side above the ears, rather like Moe of the Three Stooges. Although the thought of my hair adorning a packrat mound had a certain enchantment, I valued my mop and was ready to do battle over it. My flashlight failing to expose the culprit and most of my scalp still intact, I eventually relaxed again. But the rat persisted, and twice more I lost treasured tufts of my headgear. I had to give up sleep, then, and sit poised in the absolute blackness with a willow swatter in one hand and flashlight in the other, waiting for the return of the packrat or dawn, whichever came first.

> PETER JONKER, GRANDORA, SASKATCHEWAN

As a field biologist, I have to say I've had my share of encounters with some nasty bloodsucking creatures, from ticks in Manitoba to chiggers in Belize and to vampire bats in Costa Rica. But the creepiest encounters I've had by far took place in the rain forests of Panama. While in Panama doing research for my doctoral thesis, I had the repeated misfortune to come across what were well known to the researchers there as "tick bombs."

Tick bombs are sometimes large numbers of ticks, from tens to hundreds, that group together on the tips of leaves. There, they wait for some unsuspecting animal—usually capybaras, coatis or agoutis, but often now humans—to brush against the leaf and whisk them away for a blood meal. Once the animal has hit the leaf and the ticks are transferred, they quickly disperse to find a good spot to bite and suck.

After you've been initiated by tick bombs, you remember to make periodic inspections of your clothing and to carry around a roll of masking or duct tape to zap up the ticks in short order. I've probably experienced at least twenty tick bombs in my time in Panama, some small with only a few getting on me, but I've had upwards of one hundred ticks looking for just the spot to bite.

But even with the disgust I feel for these things, there is an odd fascination for them. I have on occasion found tick bombs on leaves as the ticks patiently await a passer-by (of course, I marked the plant with flagging tape to avoid getting bombed as I walk by on subsequent days). I've watched over several days as these ticks vie for position on the plant, moving to the farthest-reaching leaf, climbing over each to get to the farthest point, their little legs stretched out as far as possible, just in case a passer-by barely grazes the leaf. One tap on another section of the plant sends the ticks scurrying to this new spot, just in case their odds are improved there. It's really quite gross, but also sadly desperate if you take the tick's point of view. But then, I've had enough bites and infections from these guys to keep me from taking the tick's point of view for too long.

> SHARON GILL, EDMONTON, MANITOBA

In the late '70s, my husband and I had a restaurant here in town. It was a terrific restaurant, very popular, but very tiny; in fact, it sat only eighteen people. One sunny Sunday afternoon in May, a young couple came in with the mother of the young woman; all were nice-looking, refined, upper class, manicured. Apparently, the young couple was engaged, and they were out here from Regina to make arrangements for their upcoming wedding.

They ordered a pizza for lunch and were all seated sipping iced tea and chatting about wedding plans, when the fellow saw a wood tick crawl out from under his shirt sleeve. The young man had been cutting the tall grass behind the lake cottage, and he and his bride-to-be started checking him for ticks. The fellow excused himself and went into the bathroom to check more thoroughly.

The mother and daughter tried to continue their chat about the wedding plans, but the young woman was obviously concerned about the ticks and went to the washroom door and tapped quietly, asking after him. He answered by opening the door a crack to speak softly to her. The considerate young woman told her mother she would just go in to help check for ticks and slipped into the washroom. The restaurant was so small that everyone knew everything that was happening, and we were all concerned for the nice young man.

Ticks are awful. They get embedded in your skin and start sucking your blood. As they suck more and more, they get bigger and bigger. It's horrible to have one stuck in you. That's what we thought, that a tick might be embedded in the groom-to-be. But the mother and everyone else in the tiny restaurant began to wonder about that assumption, especially when we heard giggles coming from inside the washroom. The neatly coifed mother, sitting alone in the restaurant booth, began to get embarrassed as more giggles and other sounds emerged from the washroom walls.

At first, the mother was smiling self-consciously as she sat there, but she blushed when she heard the sounds emanating from the washroom. Finally, she took a deep breath and went to tap on the men's room door. She spoke quietly and firmly, and then resumed her seat. Soon, her daughter and future son-in-law, flushed and smiling, emerged from the washroom. It was the sweetest tick encounter of any kind I've ever witnessed.

> DONNA CARUSO, FORT QU'APPELLE, SASKATCHEWAN

It was 1978, and I was a twenty-five-year-old nomad, travelling in Europe. I had successfully concluded my first major relationship (okay, she left me for an older woman, but anyway it was over), and I was ready for anything.

First came Minni, a shy, romantic Italian, with whom I shared almost no vocabulary in either of our languages. Instead, we spoke in gestures, smouldering looks and our common language, French. It functioned for us as *la langue d'amour*. I stayed on for two weeks when my friends left Milano for England, promising to meet them later.

But Minni seemed to wilt on the journey north to England. She withdrew into herself like a southern flower denied the sun. She didn't stay long in our council apartment squat in Brixton (abandoned by an Australian woman who left without telling the authorities). But there were enough other women in this place to necessitate friendly sleeping arrangements. Gina and I fell into bed for convenience and ended up enjoying a great deal of friendly passion. She was a young American woman living in Milano, joining the summer pilgrimage to northern climes. We had a lot of fun together, but we were not in love.

Or so I told myself reassuringly when I met the Valkyrie-Amazon Ingrid. The whole international group staying in Brixton had migrated to Denmark to pay a visit to the famous women's summer camp on the island of Sayroo.

Ingrid and I fell into lust with a bang, under the full August moon gently rising over the North Sea. She had eyes only for me, and I for her. I hoped Gina was okay with it, but, in my youthful cruelty, I never even talked to her about it until months later, when she could shrug it off nonchalantly.

Ingrid was so smitten with me that she orchestrated a drive-away vw van for our journey back to Italia, where I had determined to spend the winter. We whipped through Germany and Switzerland, a huddled mass of women from Italia, Germany, the United States, France, Denmark and Canada.

Unfortunately, once in Milano, my lust for Ingrid quickly diminished as relationship issues reared their ugly heads. This was no longer romantic. Alas, the summer was over, and it was time to settle down to some semblance of real life. Ingrid departed, tearfully, but with a sense of inevitability.

I often look back on that summer and admire my own bravado while cringing at my carelessness. I wouldn't do it again quite like that, but every summer I feel that heat and wonder if a summer fling (just one, thank you) might come my way.

> MAURA VOLANTE, OTTAWA, ONTARIO

I was born and raised on a dairy farm in southwestern Ontario. In the early '70s, I was hauled off to homestead in Fort Fraser, B.C. As lovely as it all was, with the log-cabin lifestyle, wood heat, hauling water and living in seclusion, it was also very lonely and depressing for me.

One day, while visiting the local doctor, I decided I had to get out or I would end up drinking myself to death. He referred me to a clinic on Gabriola Island, and I went there for a five-day "come alive" seminar. One of the men who was also in attendance asked, when the course was over, if I'd like a ride to Victoria. He had a silver Cabriolet vw. We drove with the roof down, listening to Phil Collins all the way to the Mill Bay ferry.

Once on the ferry, he took off my shoes, and, for the first time in my life, I had a foot massage. It was May, and the smell of lilacs, oysters and diesel from the old ferry drifted in and out of my mind. The boat docked at Brentwood, and I never went back to Fort Fraser. I stayed on Vancouver Island, where I lived with the foot massager for a year, then traded him in for his brother. Life has been a trip ever since.

> DEBORAH GRAY, SIDNEY, BRITISH COLUMBIA

I had worked in this company for about six months and the holidays were
fast approaching (as was the office Christmas party). I was a whopping
nineteen years old, and this was my first full-time job out of high school (saving money for higher ed), and, thus, it was my first office Christmas party. I
really had no idea what to expect. In my own obviously naive mind, I figured
it was going to be a drag. A bunch of middle-aged people standing around
talking shop, having a drink or two and some finger food. Whoopee! I
thought.

The afternoon of the party arrived, and, after helping with the set-up of
the bar and food tables, I myself began to imbibe. A drinky-poo here, a
drinky-poo there, and, pretty soon, I was trounced. I've never been a "sick"
drunk but I do tend to visit the ladies' room quite a bit, so off I toddled to the
loo. The one on our floor was full so I trucked on up a flight of stairs to the
next floor, figuring it'd be pretty empty. In I go, the very last stall (always my
choice) and begin to do my business.

Here I am, drunk at my first office Christmas party, I thought, and
rested a moment on the toilet-paper holder (they're good for resting your
head when you need to take a nap, too). The world was spinning wildly
around me, when I heard the bathroom door open, then the shuffling of
feet, then voices. A female voice, and, wait...a *male* voice, too! By what
they were saying and the slurpy kissing sounds I was privy too, I knew
they hadn't come in to relieve themselves. Well, not in the traditional sense,
anyway.

So I sat there. I didn't know what to do! I was nineteen years old and I knew
that male voice! It was my boss! I plugged my ears. I could still hear them. I
tried to find a happy place. It didn't work. Zounds! I was stuck listening to my
boss boinking some female exec on the bathroom counter while I sat, panty-
hose around my ankles, praying not to be discovered. When everything had
come to a climax—sorry, couldn't resist—there were some quick words of
endearment, some zipping and shuffling of clothes and feet, then nothing.

Blessed nothing. I waited just a few minutes longer, then got the heck out of there and went directly home, did not pass go, did not collect $200.

The first week of January, holidays over, I had to set up a meeting between my boss and a client. I set up everything in his office as requested (files, coffee, etc.) and, having been told to make the client comfortable when she arrived (as my boss would be late), I sat and waited. Well, from the moment those red boots came striding down the hall, I knew. It was her! I knew, because I'd seen her you see? Well, not *all* of her, but I had definitely seen those boots! Never could I look that woman in the eye.

And that's my story. There have been a few more (especially since I joined the military), but we won't go there. Might threaten national security.
> LESLEY RIDGWAY, TRENTON, ONTARIO

As the younger sister of two older brothers, I was always delegated to the back seat of the toboggan. As most back-seaters will know, you're extremely lucky if you make it the entire way down the hill without spilling off the back in a less than graceful lurch, tumble and splat. Snow up your jacket, snow down your pants, snow in your face. Remember?

Well, in our family, the back seat on the toboggan held yet another element of humiliation, one which involved our family dog, Sam.

Sam was a large male golden retriever who, for some reason, was aroused by the sight of children and toboggans in full flight. He would wait at the top of the hill until we picked up sufficient speed to fulfil his sled-lust, and then he would race down after us, nipping at the toque of the unfortunate back-seater. It wouldn't have been so bad if it were just the toque that he was after, but, sadly, the toque nibble was just a bit of foreplay for him. His ultimate goal lay at the bottom of the hill, where, as the toboggan coasted to a stop, Sam would hurl his 90 pounds of excited dogginess upon the helpless back-seater (that would be me) and hump them hatless.

Once I got a little smarter and braver, I would leap willingly from the back seat about halfway down the hill and watch with glee as my brothers rolled and scrambled desperately, and fruitlessly I might add, to escape Sam's slobbery passion.

> KELLY WALKER, HALIFAX, NOVA SCOTIA

My wife and I had graduated from college the previous year and, upon getting meaningful work, had gone out and bought our dream car: a 1972 BMW 2002, a beautiful shiny chrome yellow, the apple of our collective eye. It was on the May long weekend in '76 when our little family, my wife of eighteen months (our marriage, not her age) and my young, year-old yellow Labrador retriever, Regan, went camping at Clear Lake in Riding Mountain National Park. We were staying with friends in their tent, a smallish affair, with room for only four people; alas, no room for Regan.

As is customary, we sat round the fire till quite late, doing all the usual fireside things, and the dog was a model of decorum, sleeping peacefully at her master's feet. Then, as all went to bed, Regan decided she needed to be in the tent as well: scratch, scratch, scratch. Our friends were not overly impressed with our dog vainly trying the zipper. Feeling sorry for both the dog and my friends' tent, we decided to put the dog in our car. In she went and back to bed we went. Regan did a bit of puppy-like howling but in ten minutes or so settled down to sleep. Or so we thought.

The next day broke sunny and beautiful, as only a spring day in the woods can. We awoke and tumbled out of our sleeping bags and out of the tent. Thinking to let Regan out for her constitutional, I went over to the car. I was dumbstruck. The dog had eaten my beautiful BMW. Both headrests, the passenger seat back, the shifter knob, all four window-handle knobs, the turn-signal stalk, the wiper/headlight stalk, both door-lock buttons: in short, everything she could get her mouth around. The interior was covered in bits of yellow foam. I can't think of a more difficult time in my adult life when I had to maintain self-control; I knew deep down that I couldn't let myself get the least bit upset for fear of exploding into a rage and dispatching the creature with my bare hands.

I eventually forgave Regan. She got into trouble occasionally again, but they all seemed rather anticlimactic after that (except perhaps the time with the butter and the waterbed, but that's another story). Regan lived another thirteen years after that very, very close call. She was a wonderful companion and friend to our family, which came to include two boys to try an old dog in her twilight years. We still miss her.

> LORRY BROATCH, CARBERRY, MANITOBA

We have a standard poodle named Cassiopeia Pas Noir. Cassie has chewed her way through a pair of ice skates, most of the basement wallpaper, the downstairs rug, numerous books (one of which was signed by the author), various clothes, shoes and toys, but it is not about these exploits that I write. Thankfully, she has now stopped chewing, except for an occasional used Kleenex or packet of cough sweets, which must work well as we've never yet heard her cough!

Her most famous feat to date is now family legend. One Sunday morning, the dog began to make nasty retching gagging noises that indicate she is imminently going to barf. My husband leapt out of bed and tried to shoo her towards the back door and the great outdoors beyond. Time was not on his side; the result of Cassie's exertions was deposited in the hallway, and she went on her merry way, no doubt feeling much better. A bucket was fetched and clean-up operations commenced—my husband, Chris, is truly a good man!

Seconds later, I was invited to "Come and see what the dog has thrown up."

I politely declined the opportunity and snuggled back under the covers. As I tried to resume my interrupted doze, excitement in the hallway rose to a fever pitch. "There's twenty dollars here, no, *twenty-five*, all in five-dollar bills." Quick questioning of all the members of the household indicated that no one was missing money. For one wild and crazy moment, I had visions of untold riches, remembering the story of the goose that laid the golden eggs; it seemed we had the dog that pukes up five-dollar bills!

I was just contemplating this ludicrous thought and its accompanying drawbacks, even were it possible, when my elder daughter (age ten) announced that she had retaken inventory in her room and was, in fact, short her birthday money of $25. Apparently, she had scattered it over her bedroom floor (as is her wont with most of her possessions, despite her parents' many protests) and, owing to the ever-present chaos, had overlooked its disappearance when first asked if the cash was hers. The only evidence of their adventure was that they were no longer blue and white notes but, rather, blue and a bilious shade of yellow, which seemed indicative that they had been consumed the previous evening and had overnighted "intra canis."

Chris (a.k.a. Dad) felt he had already acted above and beyond the call and suggested that if elder daughter (Clare) wished to exchange the dog-tainted money for serviceable currency, she would have to do it herself. Somewhat reluctantly but spurred on by the necessity of redeeming her twenty-five bucks, Clare approached a teller and loudly announced, "My dog sicked this up." The lady looked askance but dutifully accepted the proffered plastic bag with its dubious contents, holding it with the very ends of her fingertip and thumb and commenting that she had never heard of this happening before. "Aren't you going to count it?" asked younger daughter (Katie), helpfully. The teller replied that she would leave that for someone else to do, and handed over the replacement cash.

> HELEN PROWSE, HALIFAX, NOVA SCOTIA

Several years ago, when Salman Rushdie was in deepest hiding, he came to Canada as a surprise guest at the PEN benefit. As the then vice-president of PEN Canada, I was involved in the hush-hush preparations for his visit, including dealings with several levels of police intelligence and security. Among the details that had to be attended to was that each place that Rushdie was going to visit had to be inspected by the bomb-sniffing dog.

So it was that one quiet Sunday morning found me drinking coffee in the kitchen with the Mounties, while a Metropolitan Toronto police officer took his dog through my house, top to bottom. There had been a few amusing phone calls about this. The day before, the guy called and asked me if there would be any problems. I said no, that we were expecting him, but the cats might mind.

"That's why I called," he said. "The dog we're using is a young dog, and sometimes when there are other animals involved, he gets, well, confused. Is there any way they could be out of the house?"

I said that I could arrange that. I also made a mental note that the next time I wanted to smuggle contraband into the country, all I had to do was pack a cat with it. Anyway, on the frigid December morning in question, I apologized to the cats and turned them out onto the back porch.

The dog sniffed upstairs and down, in every nook and cranny, while the cats hung around outside the door, making pathetic faces and trying to tell me that it was f-f-f-r-r-r-e-e-e-z-z-z-ing out there. The dog did, truth be told, get a bit overexcited when he was inspecting the kitchen and caught sight of them, but soon the job was done, the dog was taken out to the car, and the cats came back in.

When canine cop came back in to get the dog some water and to give us the all-clear on the house, he handed me his card. I thanked him and made some joke about knowing where to go next time I wanted the house swept for bombs.

"Actually," he said, looking extremely sheepish, "you may need the number. It's just that the dog, well, he's never done anything like this before, but in the dining room, well, he kind of jumped up on the table, and you may need to get it fixed. We would reimburse you, of course."

Sure enough, across the polished surface on the dining-room table were several quite noticeable sets of claw scratches. But I never got it fixed. It's too much fun to tell guests, "Sorry about the scratches. The bomb-sniffing dog, you know... "

> ALISON GORDON, TORONTO, ONTARIO

Two very different men taught me to tie a tie—my father and Pierre Berton. At the tender age of eleven, I was shipped off to a very proper British boarding school. The whole experience was extremely disorienting for a very Canadian little girl, but amidst all of the strange food, funny accents and different landscapes, I felt a curious sense of comfort and competence when I tied my school tie each morning.

On the first day of term, my father had hurriedly and patiently taught me to tie a snappy little half Windsor, and for five years, every morning before school, I found myself in front of the mirror fiddling with my tie, just as I had watched my father do each day before he left for work. Though we were thousands of miles apart, I felt a daily link with my dad as I tightened my tie and headed off to face the day.

When I left England, I thought my tie-wearing days were over. But one day, when I was in my early twenties, I noticed that my father was throwing out several old silk bow ties. The material was soft and lustrous, the colours rich. I asked Dad if I could have some of the ties, and he again patiently taught me to tie a tie—this time a bow tie.

A year or so later, while I was enjoying a brief and rather inglorious career as a radio host, I had the honour of interviewing Pierre Berton. I was extremely nervous. Pierre Berton was one of my father's favourite writers, and the thought of an inexperienced journalist like myself interviewing one of the country's most experienced newsmen was enough to give me the vapours.

On the day of the interview, I thought to honour both Pierre Berton—the inveterate bow tie wearer—and my father by wearing one of my dad's bow ties. Unfortunately, tying a bow tie is both an art and a science, and I had completely forgotten the complicated manoeuvres required to produce one of those simple-looking knots. Unwilling to abandon my plan, I tied the material into a little bunch around my neck and hoped that I looked suitably bohemian and journalistic.

It must have driven Pierre mad. Throughout the interview, he was unfailingly kind and he carried the whole conversation—a necessity, as I was completely tongue-tied. He managed not to say anything about my mangled tie until the end of the interview, but then he just couldn't resist. "Would you like me to show you how to tie that?" he said. I still don't remember how to tie a bow tie, but I have a vivid memory of sitting in a cramped little audio booth in Calgary, getting a tie-tying lesson from one of the greatest bow tie wearers of all time.

> LAURIE COOPER, WHISTLER, BRITISH COLUMBIA

When I was a little girl, in the 1950s, I took art classes at the Montreal Museum of Fine Arts. Arthur Lismer was the director then, and, although he was not my teacher, he would fly through the studios occasionally and look at all the students' work. I knew he was a great man. My mother had told me so. Therefore, I was a little in awe of him. My memory is of an intense, agile, tall, thin man in a light-coloured three-piece tweed suit and a tie—always a tie.

One day, not long before Christmas, he blew into our classroom. He stopped in front of me, examined me and asked if I would like to be in a Christmas tableau. I was flattered by his attention but disappointed to be cast as a page in this re-enactment of a mediaeval Nativity painting. Then again, I had never been Mary in a Christmas pageant: my haircut ensured that, and it probably also ensured my participation in Lismer's production. I had a Dutch cut, and in my navy blue painting smock with red bow, I must have looked quite like a mediaeval page.

I was told to go home and make a short skirt like a page's—he showed me a picture—and to be sure that I made it myself. I told my mother this and I guess she couldn't accept that I would stand up in front of Montreal in a skirt of my own making. So she made it for me. It was blue corduroy with a wide purple grosgrain belt. I wore it with stockings and my smock.

Back at the museum during rehearsal, Mr. Lismer asked me if I had made my skirt myself and was annoyed, and I was embarrassed, when I said no. Oh, the helplessness of childhood! We rehearsed. It wasn't hard: we just had to get into position and not move. This he emphasized over and over.

The big day came. We were in a large room in the museum, an auditorium I think, and it was filled with people standing waiting for the Arthur Lismer Christmas painting to be unveiled. We got into our places and were reminded again: *Do not move, no matter what!* The curtains opened and the light shone down on us. I remember it as a beautiful glow. I gazed down at the Holy Family, still slightly jealous of Mary, but nonetheless transported. Beyond them, I could see a mass of still faces in the semi-dark, focussed on our scene. I really felt part of a painting—a part even of the Nativity.

After hushed noises of approval from the audience, the curtains began to close. They closed halfway, then stopped. We waited and waited, but they were stuck. We didn't move a muscle. We just waited for those curtains to close. But it must have become too much for Mary, because she reached up out of that painting, over the head of the Son of God, and pulled the curtains shut!

Just off stage, I could see and hear a stifled explosion from the great man.
> C.R.

My name is Lance Anderson and I was the pianist with the Mr. Dressup touring show. I was part of his retirement tour. People would line up one hundred deep, in the cold of northern Alberta or the chill-to-the-bone rain of Newfoundland, just to say good-bye. In most cases, there would be a good percentage of teenagers. No matter how "tough" or "cool" they were, all cynicism would vanish. Spiked green-haired punks, baggy-panted skateboarders or black-clad "Goths" would all line up to touch the tickle trunk, and many would ask for a hug. Ernie was especially fond of these teens, "graduates" from his show, and was never put off by their appearance. The respect was always very mutual.

Ernie was a very funny man with a quick wit. He and his manager, Don Jones, were incurable practical jokers. We have all been on the wrong end of truly elaborate and hilarious jokes from these two. It was always a shock to be taken in by Ernie, because in order for them to pull off the joke, Ernie, Mr. Dressup remember, would earnestly conspire and add to the deception. It was an unfair advantage! To be conned by Mr. Dressup! Nobody saw it coming.

After sitting behind Ernie for many years, watching all his shows, I came to realize what a consummate artist he was. As all great performers do, he made it look easy. It was a measure of the man that he even took suggestions from me, a "know-nothing musician," as he would say in his best Shakespearean thespian voice. He would feign indifference to my ideas but, after considering them, would try them out in the next show. If they got a laugh, he would give me the thumbs-up from behind his back. If not, I could expect to receive a whispered, "You're fired," from behind the curtain as he crossed backstage.

We started every show with me playing the theme, on the piano. From the first notes, there would be a high-pitched cheer, and the hall would be electric with magic in the air. It felt like I was playing an intro for Santa Claus. It was very nerve-wracking to play that theme as a performer. Sort of like singing the national anthem, where everyone knows the words... no room for faking it. I couldn't make a mistake.

I have such wonderful memories of those tours, easily the best I have ever been treated on the road. We would play golf, bowl for dollars, scratch losing lottery tickets and stay up most nights just enjoying each other's company. Ernie was a good man. And if this experience has taught me one thing, it's that good men do make a great difference in people's lives.

> LANCE ANDERSON, ORILLIA, ONTARIO

In the early '70s, I was a student at the Royal Academy of Music in London, England. I was studying voice at the tender time of maxi dresses and bare feet. No money, but friends who were willing to share homemade yoghurt, yeastless bread and paper towel–hatched bean sprouts.

One bright autumn day, I felt that I was due for some luxury. What to do? More free painting exhibits or maybe a respite in Westminster Abbey, where I could trace the patterns of other people's lives—mostly men, I noted. Instead, I counted my shillings and decided to eat out. This was a big deal for me. Tuck away my Canadian accent under a downturned gaze and approach the door to a very classy restaurant.

No tables left, only a long copper bar with high-backed stools. One place left, next to a gentleman with a goodly amount of white hair. He was dressed impeccably: suit, tie, vest and watch fob. He asked me if I had ever eaten in this establishment before. I shook my head shyly, trying to keep my distinctly Canadian accent to a minimum. I had found that silence usually did the trick. However, this charming, old world gentleman soon parted me from embarrassment. He found out what I was doing in London and then proceeded to order what he thought to be the finest food on the menu. Scampi. What was that? My poor Nanaimo mind boggled.

I could hardly taste the food when it came, because my friend talked of music and culture and literature and travel. At the end of the meal (he paid), he held out his beautiful hands and said, "I'm Rubenstein." Then he laughed softly and said, "Not the one that sells makeup." Even as he left, I knew that I had been in the company of greatness. Humility and laughter—a fine combination for a life, along with my first taste of haute cuisine.

> JUDE NEALE-BILTON, BOWEN ISLAND, BRITISH COLUMBIA

Back in 1970, my husband and I were living in a Glasgow tenement apartment on the first floor. On the top and fourth floor lived a bunch of university students. One night in the small wee hours, we were wakened by some very strange sounds echoing up the close and the concrete spiral staircase. The students, on their return home from the local, were moving in a piano. The grunts, bongs and clangs as they heaved and manoeuvred the heavy burden bounced off the walls. As they achieved each landing, they rested and gave the residents of the close a small concert. No doubt they also took a wee sip of the water of life, too.

It took them at least half an hour to attain the lofty heights of the fourth floor. The third-floor tenant, a headmistress at a local school, was roused from her bed and came out to give them a bollocking. The rest of the haul up the stairs was done with a lot of giggling and shushing. There was not much sleep for anyone for a while, as once the students got the piano into their apartment, they continued partying, only stopping when the police were called in.

> R.M.

My wife, Michele, is a pianist and teacher. I am neither, but ten years ago, I was able to pass myself off as a teacher sufficiently to enable us to travel to southern Africa under the auspices of World University Services of Canada. We were posted to teach in a small community school on the northern border of Botswana, where Botswana meets Zambia, Namibia and Zimbabwe. For two years, we lived in a *rondaval*. We had elephants in the garden and baboons in the outhouse. What we lacked was a piano. That is, until we received word from a Canadian friend in the capital city of Gaberone that a British ex-pat was moving home and had one for sale. All arrangements were made sight unseen from 1000 kilometres away. We scraped together enough *pula* (Botswana's currency—the word literally means "rain") and we were off. The trip south took two days, as our thumbs were in good working order for getting lifts from passing vehicles.

Gaberone was finally reached. Arrangements were all made. A small pickup was borrowed from a Canadian. Lots of help was found to load and wrap the piano. Multiple layers of blankets and plastic were necessary to protect it on its 1000-kilometre journey home in the heat—and possibly rain—of the African bush.

When we got back to our little rondaval, the piano was unloaded with great excitement and fanfare. Students were invited in small groups for a demonstration. They giggled and cheered at Michele's playing. They were truly startled at its volume. We were truly startled at their most common question: "Ah! Ah! Ma Brown! Where are the batteries?"

> M.B.

For years, my mother had wanted my husband and me to take the piano which had been sitting in her living room for three decades and which she had previously received from my aunt and uncle. My husband had other dreams, until he finally realized a baby grand didn't fit our living room or our budget. We made plans to drive three hours to get it from her one September weekend. We arrived and easily loaded it into the back of our pickup truck. My husband tarped it with our tent fly, and, although I had some doubts about the value of such thin protection, he convinced me it would be fine. We were to leave very early the following morning, with my mom and kids following a few hours later. We went to bed, knowing the piano was safe and snug.

That night, it poured. And it poured all the way home. I was foolishly hoping that travelling at high speed would help keep the moisture off the piano, but when we arrived home and removed the tent fly, most of the piano's finish came off with it. When we pressed middle C, an entire octave went down with it. I was physically ill. But knowing my mom was only a few hours behind us left no time for hysterics. We moved the piano into its permanent spot, ripped it apart and set all the keys on the dining-room table. We got out every piece of sandpaper and every can of stain and wax and oil that we owned and set to work. When my mom arrived, the piano looked as good as its forty or so years, and the keys "had been removed for cleaning." We got through that visit without her finding out.

After letting the keys dry for a few weeks, and with my husband's whittling expertise, the piano was back on its little wooden feet. My daughter is taking lessons, and my husband plays it constantly. I think it holds no grudges, as it is now played and loved.

> KAREN SINCLAIR, CREMONA, ALBERTA

Back in the early '60s, several of my closest friends and I made frequent visits on summer weekends to a cottage located at Hunter Lake, just outside Saint John, New Brunswick. John, our host and owner of the cottage, provided many entertaining evenings of laughter, food and music. Someone had donated an old upright piano that became a fixture at the cottage for many years. Unfortunately, it desperately lacked tuning, and twenty of the eighty-eight keys were totally unresponsive. Despite the handicap, we managed to have many hilarious singsongs that continued late into the night.

One evening, after the usual choral ritual, John announced, "That's it! Tonight, the piano goes into the lake." No one questioned John's decision. In fact, it seemed like a great idea. So, like professional pallbearers, we ushered the old crock out the cottage door and rolled it off the wharf into the calm waters of Hunter Lake. Surprisingly, the piano failed to sink. It tipped on its end with one corner rising above the water like an iceberg in the North Atlantic. Gradually and peacefully, it drifted out into the middle of the lake and within a day or so had travelled about a half mile around a bend in the shoreline. There it stayed, about a stone's throw from land.

For weeks, it remained afloat, and John invited unsuspecting guests with the greeting—"Would you like to see my piano?" Little did they know that the tour involved a boat ride that ended with a ceremonial salute to the abandoned instrument. By the end of the summer, the old piano that had brought us so much laughter had slipped totally beneath the water, silenced forever but not forgotten.

> BOB MCKINNEY, QUISPAMSIS, NEW BRUNSWICK

My grandmother Josephine Morrison was a piano teacher. When she married my grandfather William Smith in 1898, she had no instrument of her own. In 1911, the local county paper ran a contest: the person who sold the most subscriptions to their paper would win a piano, delivered from Montreal. My grandmother rose to the challenge. She and her husband travelled as far as foot, horse and buggy would convey them that summer, and, the night before the winner was announced, Grandma and Grandpa drove the horse and buggy to Truro, some 16 miles away, to overnight in a hotel.

She did win the contest, and a piano was delivered to the nearest railway station, East Mines, some 6 miles north of the farm. They took a team of horses to bring the package home. It was a Willis upright, and heavy enough in its own right, but it was packed in a custom-made oak box which must have added another 300 pounds to its bulk. One of the horses collapsed from pulling the massive weight and died before making it home. Another team successfully brought the upright instrument to its home the next day.

Yes, the instrument is still in use, and it fostered my sister's career as a pianist; the piano box is also still in use, as a storage container in the tractor shed. When we renovated and had to move the piano outside, its excessive weight nearly brought us to turn it into firewood.

> LINDA M. GIDDENS, GREAT VILLAGE, NOVA SCOTIA

My uncle Rolland was visually impaired from the time he was a baby. However, he didn't let that stop him from doing what he wanted to do. He had a lot of musical talent and decided to become a piano tuner as a profession. He was accepted at a school in Seattle in the early 1950s, but one condition of entry was that he provide all his own piano-tuning tools. These tools are quite a specialized set, and they are not cheap. Because my grand-parents didn't have a lot of money, the cost of the tools turned out to be quite a hurdle.

About that time, my parents went from Kansas to Southern California on a trip. My mother had heard about the famous *Queen for a Day* radio show host-ed by Jack Bailey. Each of four contestants selected for the show was allowed to ask what they would wish for if they were "queen" for one day. The audi-ence then voted for the best request. My mother decided to try to get on the show with her wish for—you guessed it—one set of piano-tuning tools.

Mom got on the show, presented her request, and won the tools and a whole lot of other prizes. We still have a wonderful picture of Mom wearing a crown and robe, and my uncle got the best set of piano-tuning tools ever made. He used them throughout his career as a piano tuner in Pittsburgh. Although I can't tell you the make of the tools or exactly what all those gadg-ets are for, my family knows to this day what an expression of family love those tools represent to all of us.

> LUCILLE CHARLTON, ABBOTSFORD, BRITISH COLUMBIA

The yellowed envelope discovered in an old file is dated Toronto, August 23, 1961. It bears a four-cent and a one-cent stamp. The return address is before postal codes. Inside is a note of condolence from Doris Weaver, a case-worker with the Canadian National Institute for the Blind. In the note, Doris apologizes for not attending the funeral of my four-year-old son, Billy, but assures me "he is now where nothing can hurt him, and any discomfort he had is over."

The past comes flooding back to me, and forty years seem like yesterday. Billy was in the advanced stages of a genetic condition, from which his sister Nancy had died four years previously. We were not surprised when Billy lost his sight but totally unprepared to deal with a blind child in the terminal stages of his illness. Also, it was to be a race against time whether Billy would die first or the child I was carrying would be born.

It was into this house of madness that Doris Weaver arrived. She quickly assessed the situation and went about educating, consoling and caring. I was quick to inform her that nothing could be done about Billy's problems, especially about getting him to eat, as he wasn't expected to live. "Well, *you* are," Doris said, "and you have to get through these next few months as best you can."

Billy's frustration with his blindness was exasperated by the fact that I sat him in a high chair in order for me to try to feed him his meals. He flung the food about and, of course, I didn't have the heart to reprimand him. He had turned from a dear little boy to a monster, and I neither had the skills nor the inclination to help him. Doris saved my sanity.

> JOYCE BEATON, BAYSVILLE, ONTARIO

PART 4

I CAN HEAR HEARTS CALLING ME FROM THE LANDFILL

The greatest compliment anyone every paid the Roundup came from a listener who said he found the show "subtly subversive." I can't remember what specific event sparked this remark, but I treasure the observation, even though "subversive" is perhaps too fraught with political overtones to really apply to our modest afternoon enterprise. Still, it might be true that a show that has truck drivers impersonating Ethel Merman while driving the Trans-Canada, or schoolchildren making farting noises on the phone with their armpits or English professors singing the poems of Emily Dickinson to the tune of "The Yellow Rose of Texas," has at least the possibility of pulling the rug out from under the expectations of a listening public more accustomed to reportage and analysis from their public broadcaster.

The Roundup has plenty of room for the whimsical, but it also accommodates the serious, even the tragic. There is plenty of evidence of that in these letters, many of which have been a struggle to get through on air, simply because I found myself fighting back tears or gulping down sobs, and I am not a person much given to lachrymose indulgences. Sometimes, this weepiness rises from unlikely sources. When I asked for stories about teddy bears who travelled, for instance, I expected we'd get a lot of sweet, maybe even cloying, stories, and I recall that there were more than a few of these. However, it never occurred to me that just as many would be so affecting and go straight to my tear ducts. I like knowing that on any given day, even my own expectations might be subverted.

When I was growing up in Newfoundland, our home sat on a steep cliff overlooking the sea. Adjacent to our property was the large Roman Catholic cemetery. Every spring, after the winter snows retreated and the first of a predictable series of spring storms had struck, the cliff suffered serious erosion. There was always talk of the cemetery cliff slipping away and exposing the coffins. Rotted coffins and their contents were said to have dropped to the beach below.

The spring I turned ten, my best friend, Muriel, and I made a pact to visit the beach directly after the first storm and search for whatever might have fallen from the eroding graveyard. We kept our plan a secret from our friends, fearing they might beat us to it. Our parents, who knew of our intentions, had been unable to dissuade us.

The storm blew in on a school day, and the cold wet afternoon that followed found us scanning the shoreline and looking up the cliff at the cemetery. Sure enough, stones and gravel had clearly fallen to the beach, and this fuelled our hopes of making a grisly find. We searched the shore for an hour before we found it. Wedged between two large stones at the high-tide mark was a hand. Nothing else, just a pale, withered hand. We shrieked, turned tail and ran, clambering up the cliff, heading straight for home.

Mom and Dad were in the kitchen, fixing supper. Hysterically, we poured out the details of our misadventure. Dad looked properly concerned but said that due to the incoming tide and approaching darkness, we couldn't return to the beach till morning. He promised to accompany us then.

Muriel stayed over—we had a restless night—and the next morning, we were up extra early and down to the beach. We headed straight for the rock, Dad close behind, and were shocked to find that the hand was gone. We couldn't believe it. The tide couldn't have carried it away—the stones were clearly above the high-tide line. Dad looked bemused, which made us cross, thinking he believed it all to be just our imaginations.

That very day, once again after school, we decided to resume our search. We returned to the beach and to the rocks, and there, wedged between them once again, was the hand. On closer inspection, however, it proved to be a latex glove lightly filled with sand.

Furious, we yanked it from between the stones. Who could have played such a trick? Away we went, carrying the offending hand, and when we came into the kitchen, totally irate, we saw right away who the trickster had been. There sat Dad, waiting and grinning like a Cheshire cat.

> HELENA MACLEAN, LUNENBURG, NOVA SCOTIA

When Penny (a.k.a. Theresa) and I were first married, in 1973, we lived in Sheffield, Ontario, in a converted church. The building dated from about 1850, and it was in sad repair. There was hay, not grass, in the backyard. I scythed it. It was Penny's job to do the cleanup with the lawn mower. She ran over a very hard object, and the metal blades sent sparks flying in all directions. She had struck an old headstone carved with her own name, Theresa Stark, and the dates 1852–1873. She had died at the age of twenty-one. Now, Penny was born in 1952, and in 1973, she was twenty-one years old.

In 1977, we purchased our first house in Hespeler. We used to walk every evening past a local graveyard, and there, too, we found a headstone bearing the name—you guessed it—Theresa Stark. I can't imagine what the odds are for this, but they must be in Lotto 6/49 vicinity.

> BOB AND PENNY (THERESA) STARK, CAMBRIDGE, ONTARIO

My mother-in-law tells of up growing up in tough economic times with strict parents. Her father was a loud man with a violent temper. He was quick to lash out, both verbally and physically.

Her father is buried in a church graveyard in a small village. On one of her visits to the grave, she said out loud, "Pop, why did you have to be such a miserable so-and-so?" Then, she felt a tug at her throat. She reached up and discovered that her pendant was gone. Her children had just given her the amethyst pendant a few weeks ago. Now, all that was left was the gold chain.

She started to panic. When did she lose it and where? She and her husband frantically combed through the grass. After almost an hour of searching, they gave up. As they were walking away from the grave, her husband saw something shining. Wedged against the headstone, just poking up from the dirt, was the pendant.

On the way home, they decided to stop at a jeweller to have it fixed. The jeweller examined the pendant and told them he was amazed that it had fallen off without being tugged, as the pendant was not worn at all and the separation in the link was so small you could only see it under a magnifying glass. My mother-in-law turned pale and started to shake. Had someone reached out again?

> D.H.

A few years ago, my five-year-old daughter was taken by a family friend on an excursion to a large and seedy Vancouver thrift store. Handed fifty cents to spend as she pleased, she chose a teddy of the Care Bear persuasion, a cheesy creation of grubby white acrylic fur, decorated with purple and pink hearts, which she imaginatively named Hearts.

The bear was added to her already overflowing collection of stuffies, where it lived in relative harmony and more or less ignored, until one day, when I foolishly left my daughter and one of her school chums alone in the kitchen during a candlelit dinner. I returned to find the room filled with acrid smoke and my daughter in tears. It seems her friend had convinced her to see what would happen if they held Hearts's furry bottom over one of the candles. A large hole with very blackened edges was the unfortunate result.

After extracting solemn promises from both children never to play with candles again, I added Hearts to my mending basket, and both my daughter and I promptly forgot about him.

Nearly a year later, during one of my infrequent mending days, I found the bear. There were so many shirts waiting for buttons, pants waiting to be shortened, socks to be darned and zippers to be replaced—well, I did something I will never forgive myself for. I took the ugly little bear and buried it in the bottom of the garbage can. Natasha doesn't even remember she owns this, I told myself. She has a dozen other bears and a menagerie of tigers, lambs and parrots.

How wrong can a mother be?

Some weeks later, I was again parked in front of my sewing machine when my daughter came flying into the room, her face streaked with tears.

"Oh, Mummy," she said, burying her face in my shoulder. "I can hear Hearts calling me from the landfill! He's saying, 'Come and get me!'"

I nearly died.

My face burning with shame, I pretended he was lost somewhere in the disaster that was my sewing room and promised to have a good look for him soon. I never did confess that I'd thrown Hearts away. Until now.

Do you think bears really can send telepathic messages from the Great Beyond?

> TRACY TAYLOR, COBBLE HILL, BRITISH COLUMBIA

I received my teddy, simply called Teddy, as a baby in India more than fifty years ago. Our family lived in the plains on the Ganges River near Mirzapur, and, during the extreme heat of the summer, we would travel by train and car to Mussoorie and the coolness of the foothills of the Himalayan mountains. Teddy would travel with me.

He was a plush bear, dressed in a full suit of peach velvet trousers and turquoise velvet jacket. He started out with button eyes, which my mother replaced with woollen embroidery, for fear I would pull them off and swallow them.

When I was two, we travelled to England, the original home of my father. He came to India at age eighteen and made it his home for twenty-three years. On that around the world trip, we visited Ireland, Rome (where my sister Rosamond was conceived), Australia, Canada (the home of my mother), Hawaii, Singapore and back home to India.

The summer of my fourth year, I contracted polio in Mussoorie, and Teddy stayed with me during my nearly two-month hospital stay. He was steamed in a sterilizer to rid him of germs before we left the hospital. After that, my sister, mother, Teddy and I travelled to Delhi, then to London and on to Gander, Newfoundland, and finally to Vancouver, where Teddy and I lived in the Children's Hospital for eleven months.

By this time, Teddy's original suit was wearing thin, and my mother sewed him a new bright woollen plaid suit. He spent an imaginative and vigorous childhood with a monkey called Yibin and various baby dolls belonging to my sister, and when I was ten years old, he shared the stage happily with the world's first Barbie.

In my early twenties, he travelled with me to Pender Harbour, where he once again acquired new duds: striped red, white and blue flannelette trousers and a blue terry shirt.

We moved across the water to Courtenay on Vancouver Island in my late twenties, and Teddy became a member of my daughter Eliza's toy collection and, seven years later, part of my daughter Belinda's stuffed-toy family, once again brother to another monkey called Gibby.

During Eliza's early years, Teddy was sewn into new red corduroy trousers. Eliza became a budding seamstress as a nine year old and made Teddy a peach-coloured cotton shirt and white brocade jacket with a multicoloured woollen tie, which is the outfit he sports today.

Teddy has seen many miles by air, land and sea. His face is repaired with tan embroidery thread where he was attacked and wounded by a dog. He has absolutely no fur left on his exposed body parts (head and hands), with the exception of a few wisps deep in his ears. His days of travel are probably done now, and, as evidenced by his permanently embroidered smile, I believe he is happy to be sitting on the shelf next to the Irish peasant doll.

> JUDY NORBURY, COURTENAY, BRITISH COLUMBIA

As children, my brother, sisters and I were "fortunate" enough to travel the world with my parents. I hesitate with the word "fortunate," because, as youngsters, we did not always see the good fortune in traipsing around the world. We followed our father through museums, pagodas, jungle treks and strange opera productions. We definitely had a different definition of vacation than Dad. Of course, as a well-travelled adult, I appreciate all that I have seen in the "world classroom," as my father would put it. At the time, I think we might have all preferred Disneyland.

There was always one silver lining on all of our trips: White Peter. White Peter was a hand-knit white teddy bear that my aunt had made for my brother. He had amber button eyes, and the cutest little pair of yellow and blue striped overalls. My brother seemed to resent these vacations more than the rest of us and rarely spoke other than to complain or tease my sisters and me, but White Peter had a life of his own. He would sing for us on the long car journeys through Eastern Europe or pretend to be a tour guide with his own quirky, bearlike outlook on our travels.

On one trip, we had been in Asia for close to three months. My father, an avid mask collector, had decided to take us to a little island off the coast of Japan to buy masks. We all revolted, including my mother. We were staying at a charming little Japanese inn and were exhausted. We needed to rest, refuel, do laundry and ease our weary little brains. My father was adamant that we all go. Tears were no use, nor did my mother's insistence (which would normally carry a little more weight). Nothing. He was immovable.

Finally, out of the angry silence, White Peter spoke: "It is my birthday and I don't want to go." After a stunned silence, we all rallied. He deserved a party. It was not fair to him. He was the birthday boy. My father didn't stand a chance. Whether he thought his family was clearly losing their wits or he did not want to go up against the infallible White Peter, I will never know. But for some reason, he relented. He left the next day on his own.

My mother knew when to celebrate a miracle. She gave us each a small amount of yen so we could each buy White Peter a present. Upon our return with tiny little gifts, meticulously wrapped by Japanese shopkeepers, we found a low-lying tea table laden with wonderful treats. White Peter sat at the head of the table, with a little rice-paper hat lovingly made by my mother. White Peter entertained us the whole day with his imitations of Kabuki actors and strange tales about Japanese samurai. My father came back to a restored family.

My brother still has White Peter. He now sits among many teddies, but he is their leader. He has travelled the world and will always have many stories to tell. As for my father, I still don't know why he gave in to a teddy bear. Maybe he is the one who needed a break from a rambunctious, and very outspoken, little bear.

> ANDREA OBERDIECK, VANCOUVER, BRITISH COLUMBIA

When I was eight years old, my parents left Saltspring Island, British Columbia, for the U.K. They had been farming on the island and planned to return to the U.K. to buy a boat, sail it back to Canada, and use it to transport their farm produce. That was the plan.

They had never owned or sailed a boat in their lives. My father's only experience with celestial navigation had been gained in North Africa, in the desert, during the Second World War, while my mother had learned navigation from a small book. They bought the boat, the yacht *Tzu Hang*, in Dover, and bought a useful book to tell them how to sail her.

They also bought an enormous blue teddy bear as a companion and entertainment for me while we three, plus Blue Bear, sailed back from England to Canada.

In the Bay of Biscay, *Tzu Hang* got into a really spectacular storm: roaring wind, spume blowing off the tops of the waves, the boat corkscrewing about. My parents, after consulting with their books on how to sail, decided to heave to, which they did successfully, and then both of them came down below to read and relax while *Tzu Hang* rode out the gale.

In order to entertain me, my father put my yellow oilskins and sou'wester on Blue Bear, took him up on deck to the cockpit and fastened him beside the wheel. We were all pretty pleased with this idea, and Blue Bear looked quite smart and very responsible as he conned *Tzu Hang* through the blowing spray.

We were all down below when the wind dropped quite sharply, and, in the sudden quiet, we could hear the thrum of engines through the hull. We looked through the tiny portholes in the doghouse to see, upwind of us, an old freighter. On its deck, peering down through his binoculars at *Tzu Hang* and Blue Bear, stood the freighter's captain.

Certain he could not be seen by the ship's captain, my father peered back at him and said, "I'm sure the dear chap will dine out for years on the story that he saw a blue bear, wearing yellow oilskins, sailing a yacht through a gale in the Bay of Biscay. It would be a pity to spoil it by appearing on deck, so we won't."

> CLIO SMEETON, COCHRANE, ALBERTA (www.ceinst.org)

It was a summer day, some time back in the mid-'80s, and I was on my bicycle, coasting down the loading ramp to the ferry, bound for Nanaimo and a bike race a few miles south of town. I wore my usual race togs—Lycra jersey, black shorts, leather cycling gloves and the ubiquitous cycling shoes. As I rolled to the front of the lineup, I ended up beside a battered pickup truck with a couple of hay bales in the back and a horse trailer in tow. I could smell the sweet, familiar funk of horses, sweat and leather. Glancing right, I saw the scratchy faces of a pair of good ol' cowboys, staring me up and down as they passed a bottle of Jack Daniel's back and forth. We made a connection just then. After all, both parties were waiting for the ferry. And they rode horses, and I rode a bike. And I was apparently ready for some brand of action, while these two—who had obviously spent the night in the truck with their buddy, Jack Daniel's—certainly had the look and smell of battle about them.

As fate would have it, the morning ferry was delayed for some repair. It soon became clear that we had time for more than just staring, and it wasn't long before I was squished between Shorty and Vern in the front of that pickup truck, sitting out the wait and listening to some predictable country on a bad stereo. My shiny legs and white ankle socks made a striking picture, wrapped around the floor shift of that dusty pickup.

Shorty and Vern were rodeo junkies in every sense of the word. They would travel any chance they could to rope steers and ride bulls. Cloverdale. Falkland. Williams Lake. They'd done every rodeo in B.C. and the U.S. northwest. But nothing could come close to the "Cal-gary Stampede," according to Vern.

Turned out Vern missed the cut to the bull-riding finals by the skin of his teeth. If he had just kept his seat on that bull for half a second more, he would have made it to the final round and into the money. Once you're in the finals, a good bull and a bit of luck could get you top money, could carry a cowboy an entire year, could put you in a whole new league of riders. Vern was that close to the money. His bull was lively. His grip on the rope was pinned. The bull made a good jump from the pen and started up with a fast right-hand spin. Vern had a good seat, had the inside track on his bull—right up, that is, to the moment when that bull dropped his head and made a quick turn back to the left. Vern's voice is burned in my mind. Like a ringside announcer at a heavyweight fight, the words rolled out from the depths of his chest, slow and loud, filling the cab of the truck with the angst of a treasure lost. "FIFTY THOUSAND DOLLARS!" he boomed. "I was this close to fifty thousand dollars!"

The three of us passed the better part of an hour in that cab. I had a sip of their Jack to be sociable, and we showed each other our scars, which prompted Shorty to launch into Vern. "Make him your face, Vern. Vern, show him your face." Vern tossed his teeth onto the dashboard, turned his cowboy hat sideways, jammed the brim down, and showed me his face. His lips disappeared down his throat as he sucked them into a downturned frown. He rolled his eyes and leaned over close and smacked his lips, threatening to kiss the kid dressed in the shiny nylon outfit. Shorty howled with laughter, like he must have done each and every time Vern would make his face.

We carried on about bike racing and horses and country music while we waited for the ferry. But if ever a lull in the conversation begged for it, Vern would reach deep and cry it out one more time, "FIFTY THOUSAND DOLLARS!"

We eventually boarded the ferry. I rode my bike into the belly of the boat and walked barefoot around the deck with my impractical race cleats in my hand. Halfway through the crossing, I happened upon Shorty and Vern again, slouched in the rows of seats on the viewing deck. The Jack Daniel's had done its job, and these boys were topping off their epic week at the "Cal-gary

Stampede" with one final show for the crowd, laughing loudly, slapping their knees, and generally acting up. Shorty was putting a headlock on Vern when I stopped by. I noted the circle of empty seats that surrounded them and felt every pair of eyes on the deck staring at us. I sat down across from them for a minute or so, time enough to say hi, time enough to dream up an excuse to move on. I had to get something to eat, I lied. In truth, I wasn't interested in being in the same row, much less the same ferry, should Vern make his face again. We shook hands hard one last time, and I beelined for less conspicuous quarters. But even from my distant seat in the cafeteria, I remember hearing Vern bellowing out his swan song for all the world to hear: "FIFTY THOUSAND DOLLARS!"

> TERRY MILLER, ROSSLAND, BRITISH COLUMBIA

Martha said we had won a prize. Steak knives. Wasn't that great, we were just talking about how we needed some steak knives.

"Please tell me you told them we didn't want the steak knives."

She didn't understand. "What? What do you mean? You just said a few weeks ago that we should get some steak knives. They're coming to deliver them on Saturday morning."

"Martha, it's a sales gimmick. They're going to deliver the steak knives and try to sell you something."

Martha said she didn't think they were going to try to sell us anything. We just won a prize. Why was I so cynical about everything? But the look of doubt was in her eyes. She knew this wasn't good.

"What time are they coming?" I asked. "Because I won't be here."

"They said they'd be here at ten. And there would be a short presentation. And they said your husband has to be here too."

On Saturday morning, Martha said she had some errands to do. But I hadn't forgotten. I had good reason to be out of the house. I couldn't possibly be home. I needed to give blood.

I got home at 12:15. Martha met me outside the front door. She tilted her head towards the house. "He's here," she said. Her face was wearing a look of disbelief. "He says he has to demonstrate an air purification system before he can give us the steak knives."

We sat on the couch as he demonstrated the air purification system. You could use it to clean all the dust out of the air. Just turn it on and leave it in the middle of the room. Its microfilters would purify your air.

It looked like a vacuum. It sounded like a vacuum. Funny thing. In addition to being an air purification system, it *was* a vacuum.

He put his hand over the end of the hose. What powerful suction.

We never got to the issue of price. We already had three vacuums. All three of them were old hand-me-downs, but we didn't tell him that. We had mostly hardwood floors, and he could see that. We would be moving to Toronto in a few months. We didn't need a vacuum. And we didn't want an air purification system.

We started getting less and less polite and eventually got him out the door with his vacuum. We were so happy to have him out the door that we didn't care he hadn't given us the steak knives.

A few months later, it was time for us to move. We needed to have a yard sale. It would be a good time to get rid of two of those old vacuums.

On the day of the sale, it rained. We directed traffic around to the back door, which went directly into the basement, and we kept our merchandise in the basement instead of putting it in the yard. The sale went well. One of the vacuums went early.

By noon, traffic had all but stopped. I had to study. I went upstairs to the den on the second floor. Martha looked after the remaining trickle of would-be purchasers.

From the second floor, I heard the vacuum cleaner running in the basement. I hoped Martha succeeded in selling it. We were asking $12 for it. It was an upright. It worked well. It was orange and had a nice long cord. This baby even had a light on the front to help you see what you were vacuuming. The light still worked. And what suction!

The vacuum stopped, and I heard Martha rushing up the stairs from the basement. She was whimpering, calling for me. I ran down the stairs to the main floor. Martha was holding her hand. Her fingers were bleeding. There was only a little blood, but already you could see blue bruises across the knuckles. She was pale and a little incoherent. She was obviously in pain. She was going into shock. I laid her on the couch and got some ice for her hand.

She was laughing at herself: "I put my hand in the beater bar. I put my hand in the beater bar. He's still down there. I was trying to show him the suction on the vacuum. I forgot about the beater bar. Go down there and sell the vacuum. I told him he could have it for $10. I can't believe I put my hand in the beater bar."

I was a little nervous about leaving Martha as she slipped into shock. But she was laughing. And I didn't like the fact that there was a stranger alone in my basement.

I went down to pick up the sales pitch. I tried my best, but this guy was tough. He was obviously interested in the vacuum, but he was driving a hard bargain. It wasn't long before I'd offered to sell it for $7.50, then $5. The most he would offer was $3. That insulting offer just didn't provide enough incentive to sell.

Later that day, I took the vacuum across the street and put it in the dumpster. Selling vacuums is one of those things that should just be left to professionals.

> ROGER CHOWN, BARRIE, ONTARIO

When my brother and I were children, we used to play barber with my mother's electric beater. We took out the beaters, of course, but the two silver casings that held the beater stems were raised, not flat like the modern kind. They spun round and round at high speed. I was pretending to shave my brother's head and his hair caught in the casings. He began to scream, and I ran to get my mother, who, as it was Sunday morning at about 7 AM, was still in bed.

Now, my parents slept in the altogether. My mother, startled from sleep, ran directly to the living room to discover my brother, the beater still churning away with handfuls of his hair in it. She pulled the beater towards herself, flicking the reverse switch. It spun backwards, releasing my brother. But it caught her pubic hair, winding all the time. By this time, my father, roused by the general commotion, arrived to find my poor mother, shrieking at the top of her lungs, stuck to the beater in a most compromising fashion. He rushed forward, shaking with unstoppable laughter, and pulled the plug.

And there you have our family's best story of how not to use a beater.

> S.H.W., SASKATOON, SASKATCHEWAN

It all began with spaghetti. My husband (at the time, just a boyfriend) had bought the ingredients for the sauce that was to adorn our noodles. With great pride, he pulled out a couple of jalapeno peppers, declaring that they were the key ingredients to the sauce. He began chopping the peppers, and it is here that my memory of the events becomes a little skewed. Maybe it was the wine, maybe it was the warmth of the late afternoon sun, but, somehow, the sauce was forgotten and we found ourselves in a passionate embrace right there in the kitchen. It looked like this was going to be more than a kiss.

Suddenly, I stopped. I stopped everything I was doing, and all thoughts carnal were quickly vanquished as I felt a particular burning (not of the passionate kind) welling up in my…well, you can imagine. It took but a brief moment to understand the chemistry of what was happening, and I yanked my husband's jalapeno-infected hand from its residency. I began jumping up and down shouting, "Bath! Bath!"

I can't remember how long it took for the pain to simmer down, but I do recall that we both couldn't help but laugh as I soaked in the tub, trying to quench the flames.

To this day, the sight of hot peppers still conjures up a little giggle, but you can count on the fact that I am very careful when handling them. Hot peppers and passion just don't mix.

> GILLIAN MCLENNAN, VANCOUVER, BRITISH COLUMBIA

My dad is one of those interesting individuals whose mission earlier in life seemed to be to overindulge in everything. When I was about ten years old, my dad drank a 40-pounder of rye a weekend, smoked four packs of cigarettes a day and never seemed to get enough of hot peppers—he especially loved to sit down with a jar full of those Bick's hot banana peppers and eat them straight. (Today, I would not think them hot, but, as a ten year old, they scared me.)

Anyway, he had developed a reputation amongst his friends as someone who could eat anything hot, and a friend decided to bring over a jar of what he called "the hottest peppers in the world" to test my dad's prowess. He and his cronies were sitting around the table, abusing various substances, when out came the jar of peppers. After the briefest hesitation, my dad reached right in and popped one of the strange, wrinkled, orange peppers into his mouth whole. Some listeners may know about the pepper I am describing—

the dreaded Scotch bonnet—a pepper so hot it is recommended you handle it only with gloves on—at least that's what I always do.

The resulting string of expletives was enough to make my ears burn (and expletives were pretty common in our house). Tears were streaming down my dad's face, but he was also laughing at himself, which always caused him to want to urinate—of course, all that beer didn't help. Sure enough, after about thirty seconds in the bathroom, there was an even *louder* string of expletives, accompanied by moaning. He came out of the bathroom red-faced, with more tears, and headed straight for the kitchen sink, where he dropped his drawers and tried to rinse the residue (you know, the very hot capsicum oil residue that you need to wear gloves to avoid) off his privates. His friends were rolling on the floor, their howls of laughter punctuated by my dad's continued howls of pain.

It was an incident he never lived down. Later that year, he received Christmas cards from his friends addressed: "Have a good one—Hot Balls!!"

My dad doesn't overindulge in anything for the most part these days—his rock-hard arteries and other ailments prevent him from that. He did, however, pass on his love of really hot peppers to me—and, because of his experience, I always handle them with extreme caution.

> E.N.

I look forward to the cold so that I can wear my Mongolian underwear. My husband and I were teaching in Mongolia mid-September to mid-October in Ulaanbaatar (the main city). Clear sunny days, on which you should have been able to see forever, were hampered by the tears streaking down our faces. It's the wind.

Oh... the wind. It usually comes from one of two directions: south from China or north from Siberia. The southern wind carried the scent of sage and an indefinable smell of warm earth. It cooled rather than chilled. Even a cloudy day with a southern wind felt kindly. The northern wind bit and tore, and it galed towards you with no scent at all. By the time your skin felt it, you knew this was gonna hurt. It made my body quake, especially when I realized that this was October after all... and winter was a hint away.

My Mongolian underwear feels silly in Vancouver. Like a damp dog, only slightly wet. The only time I think it will come in useful is on January 1 in English Bay for the Polar Bear Swim.

> MRS. CAROLE VOSBURGH, NORTH VANCOUVER, BRITISH COLUMBIA

When my father died, he was living alone in Surrey. The job fell to me, the eldest and only daughter, to travel from Ontario to empty out his apartment and dispose of all his personal effects. There was no funeral and no body to attend to, as his religious relatives had whisked his physical remains away before my plane even landed in Vancouver.

It is a sad job to make disappear all the traces of someone's life. My mother flew from Edmonton and helped with the administrative details. I sold his furniture on consignment, gave his dishes to Goodwill, took his medications back to the pharmacy, and packed up the clothing and personal items I thought my brothers might want to keep. Most of his clothes were not my size or style, but I kept a few things: the wool dressing gown I had sewed for him as a Christmas present; the Kashmiri vest, bought before I was born on my parents' travels in India; and his most recent silly hat, a cheap tweed cap that he wore during one of our last visits. I also happened across a couple of pairs of perfectly good, almost new, men's cotton underwear—your standard Stanfield's. I don't know what possessed me, but I kept those as well.

A few years later, on a day when I was fresh out of clean laundry, I dug out a pair of my dead dad's underwear and put them on. Now, perhaps I have lived a sheltered life, but until that day, I had never tried on men's briefs. I was amazed at how comfortable and, well, sturdy they were! They seemed much better suited to the rigours of womanhood than the skimpy, binding and stupidly named "panties" I'd been wearing all my life.

At first, I wore my dad's gotch only in laundry emergencies or around the house. Gradually, I grew bolder, and they became part of my regular wardrobe. Lately, I have forsaken women's underwear altogether and buy only men's. Strictly a matter of comfort, you understand! I'm not sure what my mother will think of this, but my father might be amused to know that now I think of him every time I root around in my underwear drawer!

> GWEN O'REILLY, KAMINISTIQUIA, ONTARIO

For a good part of the year, I ride my bicycle to work. In order to facilitate this process, I usually carry my clean clothes to work and shower and change once I get there (I am certain that my colleagues appreciate this). My routine is to arrive early, lock up my bike, take the elevator to my cubicle on the third floor, unpack my clean clothes, and go back to the ground floor to shower and dress. Then I return to my cubicle.

On one particular morning after I had showered and was dressing, I discovered, much to my surprise and annoyance, that I must have forgotten my underwear! I went through several scenarios in my mind—I was certain that I had not forgotten my underwear! Anyhow, being an innovative sort, I decided I would go "commando" that day. Imagine my surprise when I returned to my cubicle (footloose and panty-free) to find my (thankfully clean) simple white cotton underwear on my desk with a yellow Post-it note affixed to it. On the note was written: "Lost something? Trying to get promoted?"

Of course, my colleagues could barely stifle their jocularity. Fortunately, a female colleague had found the wandering briefs lying strategically in front of my director's office! I was in luck, as he had yet to arrive. The story spread like wildfire through the department, and everyone heard of it, including the director. I had to laugh as well. My colleagues still remind me of this event every so often.

> NICOLE T. LEWIS, OTTAWA, ONTARIO

In the late 1980s, a friend was employed by a producer of feminine hygiene products. He worked packaging maxi-pads. The job was a huge embarrassment to his manliness, the pay was negligible, and the heat, oh the heat! At the end of his student employment tenure, he exploded with an inappropriate action so tormenting that it remains in the realm of urban legend to this day. On his last shift, he carefully opened one of the boxes, removed and opened a single maxi-pad, and carefully wrote on it with a large indelible black marker: "HEY LADY!"

He then replaced the pad in its box, resealed it and packaged it in a carton for shipping. We waited for weeks to hear of the resulting lawsuit but were relieved not to hear reports of frightened women receiving messages in this most personal of ways.

> C.D. STEWART, TILLSONBURG, ONTARIO

My mother taught me to iron in Glasgow, Scotland, in the 1950s. Mondays were washdays come hail or shine. Winter, spring, summer or fall, the clothes were always hung outside.

"You can't beat the smell of clean sheets dried outside," she professed, and

I do agree with her, despite the fact that these sheets often ended up on the "pulley" above the kitchen table where we ate most of the time. This "pulley" was a device made out of wood and rope: damp, sometimes frozen, clothes were hung there in the winter to finish drying. Many a watery meal was consumed at that table.

Ironing occurred the following day, took several hours and was a great source of pride to my mother. To this day, and my mom has been with the angels for many years now, I iron religiously after every wash. Shirts are my pride and joy: collar, cuffs, sleeves, front without buttons, back and second front with buttons.

When I moved to Canada in 1970 and had my first child a few months later, my mother's lessons stayed with me, and all my wee bairn's diapers were duly ironed before being applied! Cloth diapers had been sent from the U.K. and had to go through due process! I might add this procedure lasted only a few weeks before I conceded that I had taken my mother's teachings too far. I confess I had to overcome more than a modicum of guilt before settling into "the Canadian way" and shifted to disposable diapers—but not all of the time, Mom.

> EILEEN CUNNINGHAM, LONDON, ONTARIO

When our first son was born, my dear hubby and I were thrilled and overwhelmed at times, like most new parents. One Sunday afternoon, my husband and I were having words, not the rip-roaring yelling kind, just the snipping back and forth kind. I can't even remember what it was about, but in the middle of it, my post-pregnancy hormones and lack of sleep took over. My beautiful infant son witnessed his loving mother wind up and throw his freshly removed diaper right at his father's head. My years of playing baseball paid off. Yes, it hit its target and promptly exploded!!!

I gasped, and my husband sat blinking at me with urine-soaked bits all over his head. I don't think I had ever thrown anything directly at anyone before, and, I mean, what are the odds of me actually hitting my target?

Yes, we are still married, we have three children and we just celebrated our ten-year anniversary.

> JILL MASSEY, STRATHROY, ONTARIO

Long ago, long long ago, when our kids were still in elementary school, I found life was getting rather stressful, especially around lunchtime. We had five kids, and four of them were coming home for lunch daily. It seemed their stresses would come to a head around the lunch table—scrapping, teasing, arguing—and I said to my husband one morning (before he left for the peaceful life at work) that I just didn't know how to tackle the situation. He suggested dropping a plate, as that was what his father had done a few times when his mother suggested a helping hand with the dishes was needed.

So, one lunchtime, when the noise and the squabbling were really getting to me, I picked up a plastic bag of milk and chucked it into the middle of the kitchen table. It broke, yes, and it spilt all over the place and all over them too; and I, now rather embarrassed at this lack of self-control, turned tail and left the house for a short walk around the block.

I'd like to say this solved the problem and they were all angels forever more. But, of course, that didn't happen. However, it has become a bit of a family legend, and the kids, now in their twenties and thirties, still remember with a giggle "the time Mum threw the bag of milk."

> TESSA CASTELL, "MAD MILK-SLAMMING MOMMA,"

ST. ANDREWS, NEW BRUNSWICK

About twenty years ago, my husband was involved with the Ontario Cycling Association and did some officiating at some of the provincial races. Our younger son, Matthew, and I went to Peterborough with him for such an occasion one weekend in August. It was a beautiful weekend, hot and sunny. All the way home, I thought about how hot and thirsty I was and how I would enjoy the two cold beers I knew were waiting for me in the fridge. When we got home, it was early evening, and neither my beer nor our older boy, David, was home. The empties were on the grass by the back door.

I was filled with a terrible fury but was frustrated by the absence of the reason for it. I went into David's room and dumped every movable object, including his mattress, onto the floor. The exercise (he had a lot of "stuff") helped relieve the rage I felt, and I went to bed. When David got home and saw his room, he went to Matthew and shook him awake.

"Matthew!"

"What?"

"Who did this to my room?"

"Mom."

"Why?"

"Because you drank her beer."

This episode has entered into the family annals and is shared with any and all new members. By the way, no one has taken my last beer since.

> DOROTHY BARTRAM, TORONTO, ONTARIO

Several years ago, I bought my husband, Pierre, a beautiful leather jacket for Christmas. Since it was purchased in the fall, I proceeded to hide it in the laundry room. One evening in December, Pierre descended to the "dungeon" (a.k.a. laundry room), where I was trying to get through another mountain of laundry. He proceeded to moan and groan about the excessive cost of Christmas, what with three young children, etc., etc., and that perhaps we should not exchange gifts, and on, and on, and on.

I was never one to expect expensive gifts. Surely some thoughtful little thing should not be too onerous an expense, I thought to myself, internally smouldering with anger. Well, that anger turned into mega anger. I had hit all of the post-Christmas sales, purchasing discounted toys for our children's following Christmas. I had saved money all year from my meagre little freelancing jobs to buy a leather jacket for my husband, and he was turning into the Grinch right before my eyes! So, I reached under the counter, grabbed the box that held the jacket and threw it at him!

"Since we won't be exchanging gifts," I said (or shrieked, depending on whether you speak to the sender or the receiver), "you might as well take this now!"

As family legends go, this one is high up there! Whenever Pierre wears his now long-worn jacket, we refer to it as the gift that arrived "airmail." And, yes, there was something for me under the tree!

> CLAIRE NARBONNE-FORTIN, SUDBURY, ONTARIO

One Christmas morning, when I was still rather young, we were gathered around the fireplace waiting for my father to get the fire going. My parents always had to have a cup of coffee and a roaring fire before my brother and I were allowed to attack our presents. They said it added to the ambiance of Christmas, but, to my brother and me, it was five minutes of sheer torture. Finally, with fire roaring, and my parents settled on the couch, my brother and I were given the green light to open presents.

We were on our second round of presents when a banging sound came from inside the chimney. We all turned around, just in time to see the lifeless body of a squirrel land right in the middle of the fire. Apparently, the squirrel had decided to make a home inside our chimney to hide from the cold weather. Dad quickly deduced that the squirrel was most likely dead from the lack of oxygen and went right to work consoling my mother, who was by now in hysterics.

"Don't worry," my dad said, "he was most likely dead when he hit the fire."

As if on cue, the squirrel sprang to life and proceeded to ricochet off the walls of the fireplace. Thankfully, though, the squirrel did not suffer long and almost instantly returned to its lifeless state. Christmas morning did not get back on track for some time.

> ADAM ARMSTRONG, CALGARY, ALBERTA

M y Jewish father hooked up with my non-Jewish stepmother and brought into my life a stepbrother, Pete, who has since gone on to live in Osaka, Japan, and marry a Japanese woman named Misa. Usually when I, a pretty observant Jew, tell people that my brother got married in Japan to a Japanese woman, they ask me, "Did they get married by a rabbi?" This always gives me a laugh, since neither of them is Jewish and seems like a the first line of a joke: "An Irish-American man and a Japanese Shinto woman go to the chief rabbi of Osaka and say, 'Rabbi, do you perform inter-marriages?' "

Anyway, my brother and sister-in-law have two sons, Tai-Hey and Yo-hey. When Tai-Hey was about four and Yo-hey was two, my brother and sister-in-law asked them what they wanted for Christmas. Tai-Hey said he wanted a Nintendo 64, Yo-Hey said he wanted some potatoes. Christmas came, and they unwrapped their presents. They had both gotten what they had asked for.

(Misa had drawn faces on the potatoes, but they were otherwise your garden variety Japanese spud.) Tai-Hey played with his Nintendo while Yo-Hey shot marbles at his potatoes for hours, both happy as clams.

> JEREMY WEXLER, MONTREAL, QUEBEC

My brother Bill and I sold holly and mistletoe for Christmas outside the old Spencer's store at the corner of Richards and Hastings after the last unpleasantness called wwii. I played Christmas carols on my violin while older brother flogged the merchandise. There was a deal between us and a trucker neighbour who brought the "goods" up from Oregon to supply us with our "merchandise." We made good money at that time after the war. My brother wanted my sister to use her skills as a highland dancer for a sales gimmick as well. Mother drew the line between my younger sister and myself: "You can use your brother but not your sister," was her response to the request. We also dressed in our oldest clothes, as my brother had all the angles figured to our advantage.

On Christmas Eve one year, we were making our way home on the Number Three Main Street trolley when a rather inebriated passenger bought our entire remaining stock of mistletoe. He ate all the berries from the mistletoe, complaining that they did not taste at all like blueberries. It wasn't until years later that I heard or read that these berries were quite poisonous and wondered what happened to that man. Had we accidentally poisoned him and spoiled some family's Christmas? Even later, I discovered that Oregon mistletoe berries are not poisonous; it is the European ones that are deadly to people. Thus, my guilt feelings over all those years were assuaged.

The kicker was that if he had eaten the holly berries he would have been poisoned, with catastrophic results. But then again, he got off the streetcar with his purchases before we did, and I can only hope that he left the holly berries alone.

> FRANK HEYMAN, VICTORIA, BRITISH COLUMBIA

There are small children rehearsing their lines for the Christmas pageant in the parish hall. There are junior choristers practising their hymns for the Christmas Eve family service. There are grown-ups trimming windows in the hall with garlands, as the early dark of a December day comes to this ancient seaside town of Lunenburg. Christmas is indeed coming. But it is coming to Lunenburg this year without the sound of the carillon bells of St. John's Church that have rung over the town for nearly a hundred years. Christmas is coming this year to Lunenburg without the familiar, welcoming light streaming from the fishermen's window in the bell tower of old St. John's Church, beckoning the faithful to celebrate within her cherished walls.

St. John's, this Christmas, is in ruins. There is not much left of the 247-year-old church beyond charred rubble and the scant timbers of her frame that remain still standing. This perhaps most beautiful of Canada's historic churches caught fire on Halloween night, and the terrible loss brought a town to its knees.

This was a structure crafted by shipwrights who gave the gift of their skills to the glory of God. This was a church with a soul of its own—a spirit that embraced all who entered. The warmth of the wooden interior; the breathtaking vaulted ceiling, with its hammered timber beams invoking the shape of a ship's hull; the gilded stars in the dome of the chancel, laid out in the very pattern of the constellations themselves; the pews where generation after generation of Lunenburgers worshipped, sought solace, rejoiced.

Since the fire, our children have become accustomed to the sight of their parents, grandparents and neighbours crying. Old men and young children sobbed openly on the morning of November 1 as the bell tower succumbed to the flames, sending the chime of ten bells tumbling to the ground. Volunteer firefighters wept as they smashed stained glass windows to get water on the blaze. Even now, weeks later, little things still bring us to tears. The sight of hundreds of signatures on letters of condolence. The smell of smoke that lingers in the ruins. The image of four-year-old Grace, her impish face for once serious, singing her heart out with the junior choir gathered in the hall. "I am the church," Grace sings, brushing her hair from her eyes. "You are the church. We are the church together."

And indeed we are. We are celebrating this Christmas season without our beloved church building, but we are also celebrating without complacency. We will come together this Christmas Eve, hundreds strong in our parish hall, where we will gather around the scorched and water-damaged altar, rescued intact from the rubble, scrubbed by teenage boys desperate to help in any small way. We will gather in this building and my twelve-year-old son, the last server to be commissioned in old St. John's just ten days before the fire, will lift high the cross as we raise our voices in faith, with hope and peace, as Christmas comes in all its glory and wonder to this wounded town.

This Christmas, for the first time since 1902, Lunenburg will not go to bed with the sacred sound of our bells chiming the hymn "Away in a Manger." But in the deep, profound absence of those bells, if you listen carefully, you will be able to hear the sound of the people of St. John's, the people of Lunenburg, singing—rejoicing—in the crisp, clear air of that holy night.

> AMY BENNET, BIG LOTS, NOVA SCOTIA

My father is famous in our rural neighbourhood for his Christmas ingenuity.

Those of you who believe the Griswolds in *Christmas Vacation* rest on comic exaggeration have never been invited to our household for the annual "tree hunting" party. I refer to it as hunting, since the event contains all the ritual that accompanies the most advanced deep-woods exploration, including sophisticated "tracking" methods for securing the perfect tree specimen.

First, one must decide on the auspicious day when all siblings, in-laws and friends of the family are able to attend (missing this event is not an option). Then, there is the round-table debate over which tree farm is best suited to our needs, with last year's choice always passed over for the promise of an *even better* tree farm somewhat farther afield. It won't be long before we'll be leaving the province to find the *best tree farm yet*. Thereafter, measurements are taken to determine the ideal dimensions of the tree, with stand and angle taken into careful consideration. Finally, all the gear is assembled, with everyone in the attending party (numbering anywhere from eight to fifteen individuals) sporting leather work gloves as protection against needles and sap, and with at least two, though often three, different saw blades in case the tree (a single tree, I should reiterate here) should prove difficult.

On a chosen Sunday no more than three weeks before Christmas, the hunt begins with a ceremonial brunch that often requires a wee nap afterward. One should never select the Christmas tree on a full stomach. Then, with much fuss, we don boots, coats, hats, scarves. And off we head to the fields for a day of arduous tree scouting.

Selecting a Christmas tree involves the most precarious of logic. Initially, every tree looks perfect, and, often, the very first will be imprinted on the brain as the most magically suited. However, one can never select the first tree, or even the first dozen, but must trek through snow-laden fields until every tree on the premises has been viewed—and judged inadequate—at which point, all agree that the very first tree was, in fact, the right choice after all. Of course, no one can remember or concur on which tree that *was* exactly, and so the first argument of the season begins. Only judicious decision-making is possible at this point, and so a snowball fight ensues to determine the winning party.

Once everyone is suitably drenched and physically scarred with a variety of snowball welts and bruises, the closest tree at hand wins the honour of adorning our humble living room, and all preparations are forgotten in the momentary bliss of having found the Tree of all Trees.

Fatigued, and believing that making the choice and doing the deed are one and the same, the hunting party begins dragging its collective feet back to the car lot. Only the stragglers are left to help hold the tree steady as Dad saws and then drags the Tree of all Trees to the undersized car that will bear the booty back to home base—strapped to the hood, of course.

It is only when we arrive home and examine the tree more closely that we discover that it is, perhaps, not the prized specimen it appeared in our snow-drenched haze. There are always a couple of obvious bald spots, the trunk veers a little to one side, and what looked like a reasonable girth and height in the wooded fields now stands high, fat and proud around us.

This is when the real fun begins. My grandmother is Québécoise, but sadly did not teach her children—my father in particular—to speak French; that is, except for the important words: the Hail Mary and how to cuss a blue streak. It is only when the always oversized tree—no matter how many measurements are made in advance—must be fitted to our humble living room that my dad's French language skills are put to good use. *"Merde!"* is only the most minor of his talents in this fine language and acts as a warm-up for what we all know is bound to come.

One year, a visiting family friend watched in amazement as my father removed first one, then two, then three layers of branches from the bottom of the tree, eliminating those portions of the trunk as well to reduce its size; and then, after a barrage of indecipherable French, when it was apparent that the tree still remained too bloody tall, hacked two feet from the top as well. It was a massacre. But, as my father pointed out, it was nothing a little tinsel and a few dozen bubble lights couldn't remedy. He wasn't quite right on that one, but we did have the most original-looking tree in the neighbourhood.

Another year, a particularly troubling tree refused to stand upright, having the most crooked bottom possible. No amount of trimming the trunk, balancing the tree or tightening the base would keep the tree vertical. Finally, with much Franglais (a special mixture of English and French cussing that comes only with much practice), my father rummaged in his handy tool kit and came up with a rubber strap that he stretched across the width of the tree and bolted directly into the wall. The tree didn't budge even when the cat repeatedly tested his climbing skills.

Some people have Christmas portraits or specially made ornaments as holiday mementoes. Our family, we have bolts in the wall from Christmases past.

> KATHLEEN O'GRADY, MONTREAL, QUEBEC

A girl I knew was training to be an operating-room nurse at the Royal Victoria Hospital in Montreal. Her best friend on the course was a francophone girl from Sherbrooke. When her friend realized my friend would be alone for Christmas, she invited her to join her family in Sherbrooke.

Unfortunately, my friend was working the night shift on the twenty-third, so she had to catch the Christmas Eve morning train by herself. However, her friend promised to meet her and, in case anything went wrong, taught her the family address *en français* so she could catch a taxi.

The train left Montreal in the midst of a blizzard, and the blizzard got worse and worse as it approached Sherbrooke. There was no one there to meet her. However, when she got to the front door of the station, there, to her great surprise, was a taxi: a rather strange taxi, with an illuminated white plastic chicken on the roof. She plopped herself into the back seat and said the only words of French she knew, her friend's address.

The driver became quite agitated, slammed the roof and shouted, "Coq Roti! Coq Roti!" She replied with her friend's address. The driver got out and pointed to the illuminated chicken, saying, "Coq Roti! Coq Roti!" My friend repeated the only phrase she knew. Finally, the roast chicken deliveryman took her to her friend's home, walked her to the door and wished her a "Merry Christmas."

> B.M.

Last summer, we sold our house in Powerview, Manitoba, as we were planning to build a new house the following summer in Lac du Bonnet. As luck would have it, we had the opportunity to rent a house for the interim, from a lovely couple who go south for the winter.

Around the beginning of September, my husband, my teenage son, our dog Duke and myself made the move into our temporary quarters. In no time at all, we were feeling right at home. We did not, however, allow Duke into the living room. The house was home to several stuffed critters. The most notable was a very large Canada goose. It sat in a place of prominence in the living room, so I deduced that it was our landlords' pride and joy. I must say it startled me on several occasions as I was cleaning around it.

One evening around the beginning of October, I was settled in the den when I heard a snapping sound coming from the other end of the house. I flew through the house, fearing that I had a fire in the kitchen. As I ran through the living room I stopped dead in my tracks when I came upon Duke standing rather proudly and victoriously beside the goose. I felt the blood draining out of my body. He had eaten the legs and feet off the goose. What to do, what to do??

The first thing I did was to phone the local taxidermist, who, as it turned out, had stuffed the poor goose in the first place. He told me he could do a bilateral leg transplant on the goose if I could get a new set of legs. I immediately phoned my son-in-law, who likes to hunt. I put out the order for a pair of large goose legs and feet. What else could a girl do??? The next day I got the call. We had a donor.

That night, under the shadow of darkness, we delivered the goose to the taxidermist. My son-in-law delivered the donor. A few weeks later, the goose was returned home, looking none the worse for wear. But now the predicament was, where to put this creature? I could ill afford to take any more chances with it, especially given the fact that there were no more geese left in Manitoba in November. The only place that it was absolutely safe was in my bedroom atop a tall dresser. You can be sure I found it rather unnerving to wake up every morning and see this big honking goose staring down at me.

Well, we did confess this indiscretion to our landlords, who, I must say, were very good about the whole thing. My conscience was clear. Well, almost.

> HEATHER ABRAHAMSON, LAC DU BONNET, MANITOBA

PART 5

I STRUGGLED TO CARRY THIS LEG HOME

Every day, I exhort listeners to send us their stories, by phone or fax or by some kind of mail; and every day, those stories arrive, always in sufficient numbers that we've never once known anything like famine. Every day, I say a little prayer of thanks to whatever god keeps stirring our pot. And every day, I reflect on the irony that I work at this job; for the truth is that I would never be a compliant listener like the talented writers whose work is in this book. I would never, as a civilian, spend my time writing letters to a program like the one I host. I'm too private and not nearly inventive enough, and, what's more, have few stories to tell. I've lived a sheltered life, bereft of reportable experience. I'm not complaining: Je ne regrette rien. This just happens to be how things are, and every day, when the mail comes in, I confront the evidence that many, many other Canadians are not nearly so withholding.

I long ago learned to suppress whatever niggling suspicion or fear might come to the fore when I ask listeners to speak of events or encounters of which I have not had and never will have first-hand experience. Tell me about your meetings with elephants. Tell me about the time you amputated your own finger. Tell me about the time you chased down a bank robber while you were on horseback. Tell me about the time you had to outrun a lava stream.

Always, the stories come in; and always, I am brought face to face with the realization that Canada is a land of adventurers and that the generous, questing and questioning spirit on which the country, as a sea to sea to sea political entity, was built, is still very much alive. At least, in some quarters.

Me, I belong to the species that might be labelled Salon Slug. I get nervous when I'm more than 50 miles from a major ballet company and am more interested in Caban than cabins; the only kind of survival exercise I could survive would be to be locked up in Holt Renfrew overnight, with nothing but a bottle of Perrier and a credit card. But it's a big country, after all, and there's room here for all of us.

This is one of my favourite stories. I sometimes cast my mother as the villain, or target my father, who wisely chose to disappear this day. I have used the story to smother my parents in a healthy dose of guilt so as to get an increase in allowance. I change the details of age, gore, setting and theme to suit my whims.

Every morning, from age six until I was about ten years old, I would get up at five o'clock in the morning to collect the eggs from the chickens. I assumed these animals were my pets. I named them all. I talked to them. I worried over their mood swings and squabbles. I fretted over them when they were ill.

One day, my mother found another chore for me to do. Apparently, some of our chickens were getting old, or annoying, or extraneous, and we were going to butcher them. As a child of seven, I did not fully comprehend the word "butcher" so I willingly followed my mother out to the back shed and spent half an hour frantically trying to catch a chicken. It never dawned on me that a murder was about to occur.

When my mother was about to put the chicken's neck onto the chopping block, she passed me the axe and instructed me to "Give it one good swing." I held the axe in my hand until my knuckles went white. I closed my eyes. I took a deep breath. Wild thoughts raced through my mind. Why wasn't my father doing this? How did my older sister get out of these kinds of chores? Would my mother forgive me if I chopped off her fingers in the process? I was terrified, clutching onto that axe. But I swung.

Now, beheading a chicken is actually a much more difficult thing than it seems. A seven year old's muscular prowess is limited, so my feeble little hands could not wield enough strength to fully slice through the chicken's neck, but, as I later learned, I did effectively damage the chicken equivalent of a jugular vein. My mother and I both sprang backwards as the first gush of warm chicken blood came spurting at us; and, as I had clumsily dropped the axe on my right toe, I began to hop around on one foot. When I paused for a moment, I realized that my mother was staring at me, pale and bug-eyed. I touched my face and realized that I was dripping in chicken blood like Carrie at the prom.

At the ripe old age of thirty, I now know what happens to chickens when their heads are cut off. At age seven, I did not know that a chicken would instinctively run around on nervous impulses after it had been beheaded. Loaded with guilt at destroying one of my much-beloved former pets, shocked by the state of my crimson-splattered face and amazed by the stunned silence of my mother, I did not notice the chicken lunging towards me. I tried to dodge to the right but tripped over the axe, and the chicken smacked right into my leg. Wild with hysteria at this point, I'm sure I fainted or ran screaming into the house or acted in a suitably melodramatic fashion.

It goes without saying that I rarely eat chicken now. The experiment in family farming soon became limited to quiet vegetables only, and I have forgiven my mother.

> JULIA CRUCIL, COMOX, BRITISH COLUMBIA

My daughter's version of the story is mainly fiction. This is my chicken story.

When we moved to an acre of land, I wanted some animals that could produce food and provide the needed manure for my vegetable garden. I should point out that I was a city girl and knew nothing at all about chickens, but so many people raised them that it couldn't be that hard. My first experiment with an incubator produced only five or so chicks. I tried again, and this time ended up with at least thirty chickens in all. I only wanted a few eggs and a little manure, and since a large number of these were roosters, I decided to slaughter and eat them. This is where the trouble started. My husband would have nothing to do with this project, so I decided to try it myself, with the help of one of my daughters.

When Julie returned from school that day, I told her I had a little job for her. I had a dull axe and a chopping block. I would hold the chicken and she would cut its head off with one blow. Julie, being very gusty, gave one strike, but the bird was still moving, so I told her to give it another blow, which she did. The poor child was covered in chicken blood. At this point, she declared, "I don't want to do this any more," so I let go of the chicken. The chicken, which we had tried so hard to kill, just walked around for a while, then finally gave up and died.

A friend killed the rest of the roosters and made it look so easy. I plucked and cleaned the roosters, but could never bring myself to cook these birds, as I could still smell the aroma that comes when you clean birds. I kept the chickens—that is, the ones the raccoons didn't eat—until the girls objected to going to school with chickenshit on their shoes. And I often wondered, as Julie went though those troubled teenage years, if I hadn't made her kill that chicken, if life would have been easier for her.

> PAT CRUCIL, SECHELT, BRITISH COLUMBIA

There used to be a column, in the *London Free Press*, called the Mary Hastings column. Ladies around the district would write to "Mary," and their letters would be printed in the column, and it resulted in friendships being made all over southwestern Ontario.

My mother was known as "Little Mother." She was very short, having suffered from rickets as a child. One of the friends my mother made through the column was a woman who came to be known to me as "Aunt Mary." You never called adults by their first names, and Mrs. sounded too distant. Aunt Mary had two boys, and, I suppose in her yearning to have a daughter, she took a shine to me and invited me to a holiday on the farm. My mother had to take me on the L&PS to St. Thomas to get the train on the Michigan Central Railway, and I was met at Highgate.

I had a grand time—helping to pick raspberries, plucking chickens, milking cows, having a corn roast, helping to feed threshers, riding on the hay wagon, visiting other farms, helping with the laundry and going to town on Saturday night. Aunt Mary would introduce me: I was so many years old and had been with them since whatever date and I wasn't even homesick.

You guessed it! After a week to ten days, I got homesick. I got the blues and wouldn't be consoled, so Aunt Mary dropped a postcard to my mother, saying that I would be on the train whatever day, so that my mother could come to St. Thomas to meet me. Would I like a kitten to take home? Who wouldn't? They found a little carton and poked holes in it for air and tied it well with twine and made a little handle so that I could carry it, and I was taken to the train.

My mother wasn't at the station in St. Thomas, but I knew the way to the L&PS station, so I started down the main street with my suitcase and my box of kitten. I met my mother part way there, cross as all get-out at having to come over and meet me; cross at my having come home; cross because I had a kitten. By the time we got home in London, the kitten was yowling, and my mother said that it was wild and to take the box out of the house. I took it outside and found that the kitten had one paw caught in the twine; after I freed it, everything was fine.

But I remember being in the house that afternoon and looking around and wondering why on earth I had wanted to come home. A few days later, my mother said that my brother had let the kitten out of the house, and it didn't come back. I believed her at the time, but have since come to realize that the kitten disappeared because my mother wanted it to disappear. I have never been homesick again!

> JUNE AITKEN, DRYDEN, ONTARIO

My parents were the original hippies, with long hair, a Volkswagen van and free love. My parents have photos of me when I was little. They're not those elegant portraits of children in their finery. Instead, my childhood images portray me with placards hung around my little neck, espousing the evils of racial prejudice and the Vietnam War.

My mother was and still is a radical, deeply involved in the feminist movement and living life like there's no tomorrow. I fondly remember a visit from my grandmother when I was a teenager. My mom decided to shake things up a little, bringing out her stash of marijuana so that three generations of women would have the opportunity to smoke up together. My grandmother and I were equally aghast, but, with a little prompting and demonstration from Mom, we found ourselves drawn into the fun. My most acute memory of the evening has my grandmother doing the limbo under the corn broom in our living room, all the time proclaiming that she may have smoked it, but she certainly hadn't inhaled.

My parents rescued me from the American Dream in the mid-'60s, relocating to the wilds of the Rocky Mountains, better known as Calgary. My dad once told me that one of the greatest disappointments in his life took place as our plane made its final approach to the Calgary airport. He had accepted a job in a place that he thought was in the backwoods of the frozen Canadian Rockies. Instead, he beheld a sprawling prairie city devoid of wilderness. But we adapted. In fact, he eventually became mainstream, only to return to his hippie look, if not lifestyle, in his golden years. He now sails around the Strait of Georgia half the year, eating off the sea and land and experiencing the wilderness he always sought. Of course, the other half of the year is spent in his very comfortable, yuppie-style condo on the shores of Vancouver Island, where he experiences life through the Internet and a television set.

How did it all affect me? The way I see it, a child can't possibly rebel against such radical parents unless she decides to go straight. Although I wouldn't call myself dull, I've spent much of my life seeking out "normal." Radical is fun, and I certainly don't resent anything about my upbringing, but you tend to get the feeling that you're missing out on something that can only be defined as Beaver Cleaver.

It was a shock to me, one day, when my father labelled me as "square" in a very disappointed tone. For a moment I felt like a failure, but then I realized that he was wrong. I'm not square. Square is unenlightened. Square is dull. Square is perfectly balanced. That's not me.

I learned from my parents that it's okay to be different, even if you're not. I learned that speaking up for yourself and for others is not only your right but your obligation. And I learned that a personal philosophy evolves through one's lifetime. I'm a critical thinker, and I think that's what being radical is all about. And that's what I'm trying to teach my daughters. It's not about how you present yourself or how many protest demonstrations you attend. It's all about becoming informed and asserting your beliefs. I'm grateful to my parents for this insight and I hope my girls are grateful to me some day. I just hope they don't figure out that the best way to rebel against a straight mother is to do things like my parents did.

> KASEY BREWER, REGINA, SASKATCHEWAN

I grew up as a "baby feminist," the daughter of one of only about eight "women's libbers" in a small northern California town. This was truly an awful little town, full of pickup trucks with gun racks and bumper stickers that said "Stop Rape—Say Yes!" My mother regularly made trips to Sacramento and San Francisco to various rallies and meetings, and I often accompanied her. It was on one of these trips that we met Lily.

Lily lived in San Francisco and was involved in various causes. I remember her as a very tall and imposing woman. I can't quite remember how it came about, but she asked a friend and me to spend a weekend with her in San Francisco. All we had to do was help her with "a little baking," and, in exchange, we could spend the weekend and she would take us out to a "fabulous" Chinese restaurant. Never before having eaten Chinese food and being ever eager to escape Armpit, U.S.A., I was excited by this prospect and managed to convince my best friend, Zoe, to come along.

Our first surprise was Lily's house. It was entirely done in shades of pink. At twelve, Zoe and I were confirmed tomboys, opposed for both practical and political reasons to most things "girly." Up close, Lily seemed even more intimidating than I remembered. I was shocked by her foundation and lipstick—clearly signs of male oppression. Within an hour of our arrival, she had us wearing aprons (the horror! the horror!) and into the spotless kitchen. Fruitcake, she said, we're going to make some lovely fruitcakes. It was my first encounter with the green maraschino cherry.

The next two days were a blur. It turned out Lily was determined to send a fruitcake to each of her many friends, and, in the end, we baked cakes into the double digits. At the end of our indentured servitude, we were taken, as promised, to a Chinese restaurant for real authentic Chinese food. A little too authentic, as it turned out. Neither Zoe nor I would eat the strange-looking and -textured food. We were more than a little relieved when my mother arrived to pick us up from Lily's.

By now, you have probably guessed the truth of this story: Lily was born Lyle and had been a truck driver in her former life.

For me, fruitcake and green cherries are associated with the mysteries of childhood, that feeling of being sure something strange is going on, but never knowing quite the right questions to ask...

> S.L.

I grew up the youngest in a family of five. My parents were children of the Depression, and few days or meals went by without us hearing a recounting of scrounged meals, patched clothing and improvisation. The sheer repetition of these stories was painful enough, but my father seemed to feel that imposing a similar regime upon us kids would somehow build character. The individual accounts are too numerous to tell, but the coming of winter brings one incident in particular to mind. It was about 1970, during a winter of heavy snowfall. There was no need for any mechanical method of snow removal, not with a gaggle of sons in the house.

Our tools of choice were some battered, well-worn snow shovels. One day in our labours, the handle of the shovel I was using broke. The shovel's blade consisted of a sheet of worn and twisted aluminum, reinforced with riveted patches. It had more value as scrap than as a snow shovel. I dutifully reported this equipment failure at supper that night. Instead of discussing the replacement of this implement, my father proceeded through an exercise of his dreaded "Harvard Business School of Decision Making," listing the pros and cons of purchasing a new shovel. Being that he chaired this particular meeting, the rational decision derived from this effort was that we would repair the broken handle and continue on.

Now, as the handle was broken and aesthetics was not an issue, my father located a wooden crutch, set aside after some long forgotten mishap, and fastened the crutch onto the battered blade. The resulting tool, something Charles Dickens would feel at home putting into Tiny Tim's hand in order to shovel off Scrooge's front porch, was, to my father, a proud example of frugal self-sufficiency. To my fragile teenage soul, it was a source of endless angst.

> MARC LAPLANTE, LOMBARDY, ONTARIO

Being the youngest of three sisters, I got third-me-downs. What a joy it was when I discovered that by age twelve my feet fit right into my eldest sister's shoes. Since she left earlier than I, to go to high school, I could wear her shoes, return them, and she would never know. All went very well until one day she came home early. I had worn a pink dress that day that so much needed the new black shoes in her closet. I would have asked to borrow them, but the answer would have been no, and I might have gotten clobbered, just for the thought.

Soon, screams could be heard throughout the entire house. No longer would clobbering suffice. She was going to kill the idiot who had dared to take her shoes. This idiot was shaking in those shoes. What to do, what to do?

My first thought was to remove the evidence as far away from anything to do with myself as possible. But not out of the house ... if she caught me there, great damage could be done before I would be rescued. To the basement I scrambled, as fast as my legs could carry me. A huge commercial-type dryer sat at the bottom of the steps, in the opening of a sort of cubbyhole which ran the length of the staircase, underneath it. I threw those shoes into the cubbyhole for all I was worth. I heard them hit the last step, deep in the darkness, with a thud. Good, I thought, no one will find them in a thousand years.

And no one did. The house was sold the next year, and my awful secret lay hidden in the basement. Over the next two months, my feet grew a size, and the temptation to borrow my sister's shoes was no longer there. Besides, it wasn't worth risking my life over. After what I thought was a safe distance of time, twenty years, to be exact, I made this confession to my sister.

"I would have killed you," she gasped.

"Precisely," I replied.

> C.H.

As was common at the time, my parents received for a wedding gift 4 acres of land severed from my grandfather's farm. The property was on the edge of a large valley in Scarborough and, with their shared appreciation of the beauty of nature, they situated their house so that it overlooked the valley and was completely hidden from the road by the cedar bush to the north and east sides. My father did most of the designing and building himself, I'm told, but I'm sure my mother contributed her share of opinions and labour to the effort.

The house started out with a modest three rooms and grew periodically, as the family increased, to eight in all. There were lots of windows, hardwood floors and a beautiful fieldstone fireplace, which is central in my memories of celebrations of all kinds. We were fortunate in that we spent our childhood surrounded by woods and fields which were our playground.

Inevitably, though, the world was changing around us. People were moving out from the city, subdivisions were springing up, and when the family was all grown and my parents could retire, they decided to sell the house and move farther out to "the country." The property was to be subdivided. The house sat vacant for some time, then my parents received word that it was to be torn down. I could not face seeing it in such a state, but my father, who had invested so much in making a home for his family, wanted to see it one more time before it was levelled.

My youngest brother went with him, and they wandered through the empty rooms, reminiscing and sharing stories. As they were about to leave, my father walked over to the front door, then began to run his hands over the wall beside it. He asked my brother to help and began to break a hole through the drywall. When it was large enough, he reached inside, down to the bottom plate, felt around for a moment and drew his hand out. He was holding a screwdriver!

"I was pretty sure I'd left that there!" he said with considerable satisfaction, and turned and walked out of his house for the last time.

> JUDY GOFORTH, LUSKVILLE, QUEBEC

I had gone into the school in early September to start getting ready for the new school year and had found a few things needed fixing, a loose shelf being one of them. To my amazement, the principal found me a screw and screwdriver, so the problem was easily solved.

The next day, on my return to the school, I passed by the principal, a jovial fellow I should add, who was talking to a woman whom I presumed was a parent registering her child, and called out a cheery, "Good Morning." He completely ignored me. Still continuing to walk by them, I said in tones of mock sorrow, "Well, isn't that just like a man. He gives you a screw one day and then won't even say hello the next."

I didn't stick around to see how he got out of that one.

> NORIANNE KIRKPATRICK, ARMSTRONG, BRITISH COLUMBIA

In 1960, I was a pupil at an all-girls convent school in England. Aside from the obvious emphasis on religious education and academic subjects, much importance was placed on the social graces, such as the correct way to peel a grape or why the backs of one's shoes should be well polished.

An annual costume party was held at the school. Attendance was mandatory. Free choice wasn't high on the nuns' agenda, except when reminding us how Adam and Eve's exercise of it had caused the rest of us to be born into the State of Original Sin.

This particular year, it was decided that the party would be held in the convent's beautiful grounds and that the pupils would parade in their costumes while dancing the minuet. Fortunately, it was a beautiful summer, as classes were frequently cancelled and all the pupils trooped outside to practise the minuet. That it was an important examination year for my class was dismissed as irrelevant by the nuns.

The theme for the party was Historical Figures. My friend Margaret and I decided that we would go as the suffragettes, Mrs. and Miss Pankhurst, chained to a fence. The girl who would be shuffling, bent, under the cardboard table in the King Arthur and the Knights of the Round Table entry, had, after demonstrating her difficulty in dancing, her appeal to be exempted from minuet duty granted. Margaret and I, being chained to a piece of fencing, figured that we had a fairly good case for exemption, also. Alas, no. On the day of the party, Margaret and I, chained to the fencing, bobbed the length of the gardens performing what must be one of the more unusual displays of the minuet.

I have never had need to dance the minuet since, but, like correct grape peeling, it is a social grace which I have never forgotten.

> J.L.

It's hard to explain to my children that once upon a time and not too long ago (in geological years, anyway), women were considered less than decent if they sported a pair of pants anywhere other than a ski slope or a questionable bar. However, my first run-in with the dreaded dress code was at school.

On a day-to-day basis, dress was not an issue, as I attended one of the three famous (or infamous) girls' schools in Toronto and, of course, uniforms were our daily attire. We wore our skirts as short as allowable, and, as we left school, we would hitch our waistbands up another few turns and walk barelegged through the sub-zero temperature as a thin sheet of ice formed from the top of our knee socks thighward. Pants would have been sensible, of course, but only dweebs threw on leggings to leave the school. The only time when "what to wear to school" became anything to think about was for special events, such as the school play night.

The night we presented our grade nine play, I dared to defy my drama teacher, who had issued a "NO PANTS" policy, and turned up in a fashionable pair of brown corduroy elephant pants and a beautiful yellow blouse with a pointy collar and a scarf around the neck. I thought I looked fabulous and only vaguely hippie-ish. My drama teacher was horrified and very angry. She told me I was not to be seen by the audience at the after-show reception under any circumstances.

I was tempted to let fly in very unladylike terms. After all, the old bag had consistently refused to give me any of the parts I wanted. I longed for Cecily or Gwendolyn or Elizabeth Bennett, and she always broke my little thespian heart and cast me as men—butlers and stupid guy parts—so why should she care if I carried the trouser role offstage as well? I can't remember what I said to her, although I'm sure it had a rebellious tone and did me very little good for our future relationship.

I do have an old cast picture from that night. I am kneeling in front, where the teacher had placed me in order to hide my trousered legs. If you look closely, in addition to my long, blonde, Joni Mitchell hair, on my upper lip you can still see the faint outline of where my stage moustache had been. I know I had been inspired by the news article I had read about the brave woman who turned up at a fashionable restaurant in a pantsuit and, when refused admittance, took off her pants and entered without them, her suit jacket becoming the shortest skirt ever seen.

I am so grateful to all my foremothers and sisters for paving the way to a much more comfortable and liberated existence for all of us.

> ANNABEL KERSHAW (WHO NOW ONLY PLAYS MEN OUT OF CHOICE),
VANCOUVER, BRITISH COLUMBIA

Little James Elsby sat in the front row. He had been in the front row since kindergarten. "Don't ask me anything, Miss. I'm stupid," he told me with an amazing lack of bitterness.

But, thought I, this will all change, what with my enthusiasm and new ideas straight from college.

I was a beginning teacher in a small depressed coal-mining village in Scotland, and little did I know then that I was to run into an inflexible wall built of tradition and scorn of innovation.

"This is the way we do things here," was the proud motto.

"No, you cannot have the children sit in groups. They should sit in orderly rows according to the weekly test results, so that they have something to strive for."

Hence James's permanent seat at the front.

"No, you can't have some children working on a modified programme. They all have to sit the same year-end exams, and we mustn't give them false notions about their abilities."

My first report from the government inspector said I was too friendly with my class. Presumably, this would lead to chaos and anarchy. My ideals were being gradually eroded and being replaced with a sense of powerlessness which left me wondering why I had bothered with college, if all I had to do was endlessly churn out what had been going on for years and years before. Apparently, the sign of a good teacher was a class of students sitting bolt upright, in rows and in silence.

Towards the end of the year, however, feeling a little bolder, or perhaps because I just didn't care any more, I decided to press on with a noisy, messy handwork project with the boys (the girls did knitting and needlework), where they were to make a bookcase out of wooden orange boxes I had scrounged from local greengrocers. In spite of the disapproval of the headmaster and janitor, two forces to be reckoned with, we spent a wonderful few weeks sawing and hammering and sanding and painting.

The end results were inevitably mixed, but James's was quite a piece of work. He had even hand-sewn a curtain, in the face of being called a sissy, so that he could store his few possessions in private. How he staggered home with it, as it was almost as big as himself, I don't know. The next day, he was first to arrive in class.

"Miss," he said, bursting with pride, "my dad says I'll be able to do anything after I've been in this class."

James Elsby may not have exactly changed my life, but he made me resolve not to be cowed by mere authority and to have the courage of my convictions when I really thought I was on the right track. This has not always been easy, and it has sometimes landed me in trouble, but, on the whole, I feel it has stood me in good stead. Thank you, James, for giving me this, and I hope that wherever you are and whatever you're doing, you did find something you could succeed in and feel as proud of as that orange-box bookcase.

> NORIANNE KIRKPATRICK, ARMSTRONG, BRITISH COLUMBIA

How many years has it been? A lifetime since I was a young teacher in Canada's north. My first years, I was assigned the "opportunity class": a small group of students with various stages of academic abilities and a wide range of ages. On different occasions, I would invite a student into my home to spend a Saturday afternoon, sharing in our family experiences.

Louie was one of my younger students. About ten years old, a beautiful smile and sparkling eyes, he had come to play. I was in and out, doing chores, running errands. The house was full of activity. Ready to head out to pay my month-end bills, I reached for my wallet left out on a table. It wasn't there.

We searched the house, thinking I had misplaced it, which had so often been the case. It was found but the money was gone and so was Louie.

By the time I got to the town's Northern Store, he was about to leave. Not wasting any time, his impromptu shopping spree had yielded an assortment that at once surprised and touched me. There was purpose here, no frivolity. His box was a mixture of groceries and dry goods. Colourful warm toques with matching fur-lined mitts, a set for his dad, each of his brothers and himself. Among the groceries, fresh fruit, so very expensive, that had come up on the winter road, and other special treats that would simply make the wish list of most people at that time. A smaller box contained a pair of shiny new skates, their CCM logo heralding the best in the store and, by extension, the community.

There he stood, denuded, vulnerable, his dreams exposed to all. My heart melted. The obvious lesson was to never leave my wallet in a situation that would be a temptation to others. The greater lesson, however, was to never underestimate the perception of children and the depth of the pain and joy they experience.

Thank you, Louie. I'm glad that I met you early in my career. I've never lost another wallet and I hope that over the years I have been a very compassionate teacher.

> P.G.

I did my undergraduate degree in Psychology and Anthropology part-time over nine years, while raising my three children and working on our small farm, where we organically raised all our food, as well as baking weekly for a local farmers' market.

In the summer of 2000, as a full-time Master's student in cultural anthropology, I was to do my fieldwork in the settlements of Aklavik, Tsiigehtchic,

Inuvik and Fort McPherson, in the Northwest Territories. I was also going to be working as the lead researcher on the Gwich'in Elders' Biographies Research Project with the Gwich'in Social and Cultural Institute.

In mid-June, two of my children and I went, by bus, from Peterborough to Edmonton, where I leased a truck and drove, for four days, to our home for two months in Tsiigehtchic. When we arrived, we went "visiting." At one home, where a woman was cooking fish on an open fire, we were invited to tea. After she put the black kettle on the fire to boil, she took a foil package from the fire and asked us if we would like something to eat. Before we could answer, she opened the foil to a culturally delectable feed of fish guts, eggs and head. I had warned my children, my son age thirteen and my daughter age ten, to never turn their nose up at anything: this was rude. I was impressed with them as they held in their eyes within their heads and declined, citing the fact that they had just finished supper and were not hungry. I ate some fish head and told them how good it was—it is delicious—but couldn't convince them to try it.

Within a week my son had found a home at an Elder's fish camp, where he spent the summer learning so much from this grandfatherly man about fishing by net on the Mackenzie River. When I went to fish camp to bring him home under the midnight sun, I found him gorging himself with fish guts, eggs and head. When could I make this supper? he asked. It was good!

One night shortly after we arrived, we went to visit another Elder. After our visit, he became concerned about how I was to feed my children this summer. Did I have some food? Yes. I explained I had purchased lots of canned food in Edmonton and brought it with me. He asked me again: Did I have food for my children? Yes, and I explained again how I had brought lots of food with me. For a third time, he asked me again: Did I have food for my children? Suddenly, I realized what he was asking. The traditional Gwich'in diet is meat: fish, caribou, moose, etc. How could a woman, especially a white woman from the south, have this type of food for her children? No, I admitted, I did not have any meat.

The Elder told me to wait. He had some caribou in the freezer he could give me to feed my children. I went to the freezer with him as he rummaged around and removed not a roast but a whole caribou leg. I thanked him for his gracious gift, insisting that it was too much. He, too, insisted. After all, I had children to feed.

I struggled to carry this leg home. The only spot I could find large enough to thaw it was the bathtub. I pulled back the plastic. The fur was still on! And was that a hoof? I am from a farm, I'm used to dead chickens with feathers on them, pigs sent off to market; but the actual reality of facing a frozen caribou leg defrosting in the bathtub is Culture Shock 101! It was delicious and fed us for many days, and I gave some cooked meat back the Elder. Going away is unsettling, but I find the culture shock of returning home even more difficult. Back in Peterborough at the end of August, it took me weeks to get used to a busy life, to darkness, to my gas stove and big house, to a bed—and to how awful our diet is. All I wanted was caribou, and my son's mouth watered for weeks for fish guts, eggs and head. Culture shock works both ways, and usually people just do not realize how difficult it is to re-enter your own home environment after being in another culture.

> LESLIE MCCARTNEY, TSIIGEHTCHIC, NORTHWEST TERRITORIES

More than twelve years ago, I flew north to the twenty-four hour darkness of Resolute Bay. This was a week after arriving in my new home of Yellowknife; I'd moved there from a southern Ontario city. Culture shock on these more northerly trips to the High Arctic began with trying to make plane reservations. Usually, travel agents didn't know which company flew to a particular community, and I'd struggle to piece together the route from their circuitous flights around the north. At first, I could barely pronounce the name of the small Inuit communities I had to visit. It also took me a while to get the hang of waiting for the "delay" during my phone conversations as the signal bounced between the western and eastern Arctic.

On one memorable trip, I was the only *qallunaat* at a long evening meeting, conducted entirely in Inuktitut. I ostensibly was there to lend my support for their work, but as my skills in the Inuit language were non-existent, I just tried to look attentive and pick up on what I could from body language and gestures. At one point, I realized the group had agreed they wanted some food brought in, and I had visions of a juicy pizza. Instead, it was a very fresh, very juicy, slab of raw meat—caribou, I think—which they sliced off in paper-thin slivers.

But the biggest surprise of the evening was how the meeting ended. In the midst of what appeared to me to be the full flight of conversation, with the group poring over maps, suddenly conversation ended, parkas were thrown on, and the next thing I heard was the roar of snowmobiles taking off. I was left behind in the empty room, still sitting at the table, feeling as though I had certainly missed some simple cue that signalled the end of the meeting, not to mention all the insights they had been sharing all evening.

Most of my culture shock in working with the Inuit and the Dene of the Mackenzie Valley has been in reverse—in looking at my cultural ways and seeing how they seem to lack a lot of the sincerity and respect I have experienced in the north. I remember being on a conference call with a number of "southern bureaucrats," in which the only way to get a word in edgewise was to talk faster and louder and constantly interrupt.

Although I am not a religious person, the Dene and Inuit practice of starting a meeting with a prayer has always struck me as an excellent beginning to a meeting, not only because it gives us a collective moment of quiet reflection but because I am fascinated by what the Dene or Inuit elder may be saying to elevate what I think of as "technical discussions" to a more spiritual level.

Perhaps that is the greatest lesson I have learned from these cross-cultural encounters—that any work that is worth doing involves not only the mind but the spirit as well. In adapting, I have had to force myself not to fill the silences with nervous chit-chat, to just let the words offered have a chance to sink in, to try to truly understand the message being passed on. And a Dene colleague once told me that the reason I wrote so much at meetings (agendas, notes, minutes) and he didn't, was because his words and thoughts came from his heart. Ever since then, I have tried to put my pen down more often.

> GILLIAN MCKEE, WHITEHORSE, YUKON

This story takes place in Yorkshire, England, in 1964, when I was just six years old. Winter and snow were a fascinating change from the rain. We dressed up in the woollen hats and mitts our grandmothers made us and played outside for hours.

This was the year two boys from Ethiopia moved in down the street. As amazed as I was with the snow, they were absolutely awestruck. We played for hours with them, building snowmen and having snowball fights. Lunch was called, so we left our friends playing, telling them we would return.

An hour later, we went to ask if our new friends could come out to play. We were sternly told "NO!" by their mother. Apparently, finding it too cold outside, the boys had moved their snowman inside and put him in front of the fire. We didn't get a chance to play with them again until the snow was gone!

> CARL HIRD-RUTTER, CHILLIWACK, BRITISH COLUMBIA

I learned to skate in 1953, at the Sunnyside skating rink on the shores of Lake Ontario in Toronto. We had just moved to Canada from the Caribbean, and I was nine years old. Our neighbours across the street had children the same age as me. My best friend was the little eight-year-old neighbour boy. I did not have any skates, but he said not to worry, I could borrow his brother's old pair. They were much too big, so we stuffed old socks into the toes and off we went. It was pretty tricky as they had *no* ankle support, but we still had fun, and I did learn how to stand up, at least.

A few months later, we moved away to another city. I did not see my friend or his family for many years. When I was nineteen, I went back to visit the family and met up with the older brother. Six months later, we were married and have been happily married for thirty-six years now. I often think about learning to skate on those old skates and where life has led me since that time. I still don't skate too well, but I have very warm memories of the eight-year-old boy who tried to teach me and who later became my brother-in-law.

> LUCY DUKE, THORNLOE, ONTARIO

I will never forget my son Ryan's first skating lesson, which was also his first time on skates—it was just this past October and was the most gut-wrenching experience. Not for him, but for me. Ryan has severe hemophilia, a life-threatening bleeding disorder. We treated him the day before his first lesson with his factor to prevent any bleeds.

On the day of the lesson, we arrived at the rink, got the skates laced up, the elbow and knee pads on, the helmet in place and shooed him onto the ice—with a quick "Have fun." He fell, got halfway up, fell again and again. I held my breath each time he started to go down. Help finally arrived, and one of the coaches showed Ryan how to get up on skates and get his balance. They quickly sorted the kids into the right levels and began the lessons. Ryan kept falling. My shoulders were getting tense and I was turning blue, not from the cold but the lack of oxygen. He just got up when another kid grabbed onto him for balance and they both went down, razor-sharp skating blades flying in the air. I hadn't thought about the risk of getting cut by a blade.

It was awful—it is not natural for a mother of a kid with hemophilia to watch him fall over and over again and not do anything. I wanted to run out onto the ice and rescue him: "Who cares if we live in Canada—he doesn't need to know how to skate—I don't." Of course, I was too afraid of falling on the ice myself; what good would I be to him then? I stood my ground and continued watching in agony: fifteen minutes to go, ten minutes to go, five minutes to go. Ryan is still smiling, gets up again, finds his balance, turns and gives me a thumbs-up. I stop holding my breath—I guess he'll be all right.

> SUE GILLESPIE, WATERLOO, ONTARIO

When I was a child, winter officially began when we could go skating on the pond across from our house. It was a gathering place for all the children and many adults, too, from the village. My mother was adamant that we must never be among the first to test the ice. I used to sit at the dining-room window, wistfully looking out at the others having so much fun, yearning to be with them and so afraid I would miss something.

It is interesting to note my mother had been raised across the road from the same pond. She used to tell how she and her brother would go way out on thin ice and run as the ice undulated under their weight. They called it "running benders.

"It was just like walking or floating on water," she said. "You had to get the ice just right in order to get the wavy motion that ice has before it becomes too hard and unbending. There was such a feeling of suspension and a wavy feeling of water. Of course, if you stopped or put your foot down directly, you would go straight in the water."

She told me about this when I was a young mother myself, and we both shook our heads in amazement. How could her mother have allowed such a thing? How child-raising norms change with the generations.

> ANN ESTILL, GUELPH, ONTARIO

In New Waterford, Cape Breton, we called the act of jumping across pieces of pack ice "jumpin' clampers." However, in Glace Bay (a mere 15 kilometres away), it was known as "scooshin"—rhymes with cushion. Legend has it that it picked up this name based on the sound the ice clumps made when you jumped on them.

Now, the grand winter activity of grabbing onto the rear end of passing cars on snow-covered roads was a time-honoured traditional winter activity when I was growing up. It was enhanced by the location we chose, which just happened to be a slight incline on the road in front of my parents' home in New Waterford. This incline, together with the tendency of rear wheel–drive cars to fishtail as they moved up the hill, made for an exciting, sometimes wild ride. However, you couldn't be seen by the driver, or else he would stop and chase you away. In New Waterford, this activity was called "hitchin' bumpers." This seems to be the name of choice across Cape Breton, according to my informal survey.

> GARTH NATHANSON, SYDNEY, NOVA SCOTIA

I grew up in Glasgow, Scotland, and we used to hitch a ride on the transport trucks. We used to call it a "hudgie"—rhymes with budgie.

> JAMES KEANEY, SCARBOROUGH, ONTARIO

Back in the mid-'70s, the correct term in Etobicoke, Ontario, for hanging off the back of any vehicle in the snow was "bumperjumpin'." We used to have so many friends hanging off the backs of cars that, when an unwary driver realized why the car wasn't moving, a mere opening of the car door would send a half-frozen flock of hooligans scattering off between the houses. The ultimate feat of bumperjumpin' was mine, and I didn't perform it in the winter but on a hot summer day. The plaza parking lot was newly paved, and I was wearing a brand new pair of high-priced cowboy boots. My friend had a shiny black Shelby GT 350 Cobra. The new pavement, the boots and the shiny street-racer just got the better of my good judgment. I assumed the position at the driver's side rear wheel well, just beside the back tire, held on with both hands and informed him that I would like him to proceed as fast as his "crappy little car" could travel.

The spinning rear wheel coated my knuckles with molten rubber and my arms stretched and muscles tightened as my boots slid forward on the fresh pavement. In a few seconds, my friend had gone through the all the gears and realized that he would have to stop fast or travel out onto busy Eglinton Avenue into midday traffic. He braked hard and I kept going, coming to a stop mere inches from the traffic. I let out a victory cheer as I turned and jogged back to my friends. We all laughed when we looked at my boots, which were worn almost all the way through, the insole being the only thing between the road and my feet when I stopped. Aaaah—the adrenaline rush!

> GREGORY ALAN ELLIOTT, TORONTO, ONTARIO

I was perched amongst some twenty passengers on the back of an *éléphant de la piste*, the common name for the massive Mercedes cargo trucks which ply the roads all over Africa while their drivers *faire le commerce* at every stop. Clinging tenaciously to the top of an impossibly varied and largely unidentifiable load of woven sacks and boxes, we careered along a water-logged track through the Ituri forest, dodging, as only an éléphant can, the éléphant-sized potholes.

Though thankful for the brief sunny break, the rainy season and the soggy road granted respite from the choking clouds of red dust, a constant feature of hitchhiking in Africa. Miles ahead, a vague red plume announced an oncoming truck. In the Zairian rain forest, the Trans-Africa Highway is barely wide enough for one large vehicle. The two Mercedes met, hardly slowing at all, swerved at the last minute and slid gracelessly into respective ditches, pitching passengers and products into the bush. I skidded to a stop, missing trees by inches. Miraculously, nobody was injured; the drivers would be there for days, arguing and rerighting and refilling their listing l'éléphants.

I shouldered my bag and began trudging east toward Uganda, noting how closely I now matched my backpack's maple leaf. From head to toe, I was red with the weathered soil of Africa; for a while, anyway. Later that day, it rained...

> M.D.

I was in Rwanda on a writing assignment, and, with everything that had to be done and all the places I had to visit, there was very little time to relax. One Friday evening, I was in the southern part of the country in a small and remote community. Because of the recent genocidal wars and continuing unrest, people in Rwanda are very concerned about security, especially where foreigners are concerned; the house where I was staying had broken glass–topped walls surrounding it and a guard on duty. I had finished my day's work, but I was not ready to settle down for the evening yet. It was Friday, after all, and even in such a remote and isolated place, I felt that somebody would know where there might be a little music and perhaps a chance to sample some of the local relaxing beverages.

As Rwanda is located just south of the equator, it gets dark at around 6:30 in the evening—all year round. Because it was dark, and because they had been told to keep me out of trouble, the guard and the man acting as my guide and translator were very reluctant to let me leave the compound, especially when I told them that I was interested in sampling some local culture. "People around here don't do much in the evening," my translator told me.

Now, I knew it was a difficult time for the country and that the people had been through some horrendous times, but I also know that there are few communities in the world where you can't find somebody, somewhere, who hasn't found a way of turning a local agricultural product into either beer or spirits. So, with a little cajoling, I managed to talk the guide into taking me to the local brewmaster.

Now, you have to picture this. It was dark: no electrical lights, no radios or televisions, just a few huts and houses visible in the moonlight. The air was warm and still, and it was silent, silent in a way that only large, empty spaces can be silent at night. After driving for an hour or so over dusty rutted roads and across featureless plains, we arrived at a small earthen hut. Our four-wheel drive vehicle drew up in front of the building, forcing a thin snarling dog to limp out of the way. With the engine and the lights turned off, the vast African night enveloped us again with a silence so profound that I found myself speaking in a whisper. After some negotiations between the guide and the owner of the hut, negotiations I am certain included several assurances that I was not going to turn anybody in but that I was just a crazy foreigner, some bottles labelled Johnny Walker Red were produced, except that the whisky had been replaced by a viscous yellow fluid, which, they assured me, was banana beer.

I had not gone to all this trouble and come so far to turn my nose up at a bottle of beer, so I poured a glass of the stuff. "How long has it been fermenting?" I asked, after smelling it and being reminded of, well, rotten bananas. It took a while to translate this question, and several attempts at translating the response, but the answer came back to me that it had been fermenting either two weeks, two months or two years: the choice was mine.

I had a taste, and then another, and after the fourth or fifth taste, the flavour and aroma became amazingly pleasing. While the brewmaster and my guide settled into soft conversation in the local language (pronounced ken-yarwanda), I leaned back in my chair and surveyed my surroundings. The stars were out in full and as bright as I had never seen them before. Small swirls of dust played across the hard ground to drift off into the warm African night, and the moon bathed everything in a bright and eerie glow. And I thought to myself that I was just about as far from anywhere as I was ever going to get. I was in the heart of Africa, with no really clear idea of where I was exactly, with people I barely knew, drinking something which had been only sketchily identified. It doesn't get much better than this, I thought. Nothing can ruin this perfect, pristine experience for me.

Just then, an ancient, rusty, beat-up pickup truck of unknown make came banging and wheezing up from a nearby gully, a single dim headlight casting a bouncing beam across the tiny porch where we were sitting. And from the speakers of this truck—blaring at full blast—was the music of the Spice Girls, singing, "TELL ME WHAT YOU WANT ... !!"

The banana beer–fuelled moment was almost too surreal. Western culture had caught up to me with a vengeance. But, oddly enough, even the Spice Girls couldn't spoil the night. If anything, their music, so terribly out of place in that remote and silent night, emphasized the rich otherness of the moment.

> OTTE ROSENKRANTZ, LONDON, ONTARIO

In 1976 and 1977, I was posted with CUSO in Papua New Guinea, to work as an illustrator at the Wau Ecology Institute. I shared accommodations with Paul, a rhododendron specialist from Wisconsin who also had a real interest in the native parrots. In fact, we shared the house with a number of parrots, some favoured pets, some just residing there for a while.

Parrots are fascinating creatures. In New Guinea, they range from the large and robust Eclectus Parrot—we had a crimson female, inappropriately named Scruff, who was very affectionate with men but hated women. We also lodged a range of lorikeets, all beautifully coloured. Paul had a favourite, a Green-streaked Lorikeet named Woodstock. Lories are nectar-feeding parrots that use their brushlike tongues to lap up nectar. Woodstock was very comfortable sitting on Paul's shoulder, in his hair or hanging in his beard. I like to think it was a show of affection, rather than a search for food, that would cause him to thrust his brushy tongue into Paul's ear or nose. Paul could take him into the shower, and Woodstock would hang upside down from his finger, fluffing out his feathers in the spray, thoroughly enjoying the experience. They were very close.

As Paul was a botanist specializing in rhododendrons, he had to go out on collecting expeditions. On one trip, he was gone for almost two weeks. Woodstock was inconsolable. He would moon around, not eating very much, not wanting to visit with any other humans, a very sad parrot. But he had excellent hearing, and when he heard Paul's old Land Rover chugging up the switchbacks to our house, he began rocketing around the house like a little missile. The moment Paul stepped into the house, Woodstock was instantly stuck to his beard, chirping happily and thrusting his little tongue into whatever orifice he could find.

The fact that Paul was dirty and hungry from his trip didn't deter Woodstock. He clung to the beard as Paul ate, had his shower and consumed a couple refreshing bottles of San Miguel beer. Finally, when it was time to go to bed, Paul extracted Woodstock from his beard and closed him into the screened-in veranda, which was our aviary. During the night, Woodstock squeezed through the impossibly small gap under the door, walked to Paul's bedroom, climbed up onto the bed and snuggled in beside his friend, now soundly sleeping.

The next morning, Paul woke up and noticed something small and soft next to him in bed. It was Woodstock. Dead. Crushed when Paul unknowingly had rolled over in the night.

Paul was devastated. Everyone was. Woodstock was such an unswervingly loyal and affectionate bird. Being a research institute, we ultimately made a museum specimen of poor little Woodstock, but Paul could never bring himself to look at him again. Sadly, the Wau Ecology Institute is no longer in existence, a victim of the Papua New Guinea government's repatriation policy. I have no idea where the extensive museum collection of insects, plants and animals—including birds—now resides. I hope the little Green-streaked Lory, with "Woodstock" written on the label attached to its leg, is in a good place. I know his memory is.

> BILL ADAMS, VICTORIA, BRITISH COLUMBIA

PART 6

FOR AS LONG AS I CAN REMEMBER, MY MOTHER HAS HAD WORMS

I'm a restless person, a drifter and a fidgeter and a bit of a flake. For instance, I've moved house twenty-one times in the last twenty-five years. This is not because I'm trying to keep ahead of the law. It's just that I always manage to convince myself that the next place will be different, that some new surroundings will alter my outlook, that over there, the grass will be greener.

Given such flibbertigibbet tendencies, I'm amazed that I've lasted as long as I have at the CBC. In one way or another, I've been earning most of my living there since 1984. The Roundup, at the time of this writing, is going into its sixth season, and while I freely admit to having days when I wonder about the wisdom of letting the moss grow any thicker, I've never once lost confidence that, even if the show were to run—Heaven forfend—for the rest of time, we wouldn't risk coming to the bottom of the stories our listeners have to tell. Small stories, tender stories, funny stories, shocking stories, charming stories, surprising stories, ordinary stories: they are an inexhaustible resource.

I'm so grateful to have had the chance to be one of the brokers of these narratives and to have had a way of participating in what is, for me, an act of secular but holy faith. Stories, our own stories, are what we're made of. They are what we need. They will never, ever end.

For as long as I can remember, my mother has had worms. Now that she is in a senior's residence at the age of ninety-four, I have worms. I have the descendants of her worms. She was a woman ahead of her time.

In the 1950s, when I was a small child, my mother and our next-door neighbour drove to Niagara Falls to buy red wrigglers from Captain Meisner. At that time, we lived in a big old house on Main Street in Markham, Ontario, when it was still a country village. She kept them in the basement in a large wooden box filled with soil and covered with burlap. They were fed such delicacies as eggshells and coffee grinds. By spring, the box was filled with a writhing mass of red wriggling worms. They were released into her garden in the spring, and some were returned to the wooden box in the fall. When my mother talked of her worms, listeners did not automatically think of them as living in a box in the basement!

It is somewhat scary to think that all these years later, I now have their descendants in my basement and live with the hope that my daughters will take on the responsibility in the future. There is some irony in the fact that our old home in Markham is now a funeral parlour.

> KENDRA NEWKIRK, HARBOURVILLE, NOVA SCOTIA

The best frugal mother story I know is from my friend Christabel. Many years ago, her mother asked one of her daughters to put the kettle on for tea. When the water had boiled, Mum went to prepare the tea. On discovering that her daughter had filled the kettle to the brim and that there was lots left over, she cried out in dismay, "Oh no! You've boiled too much water! Now I'll have to make Jell-O!"

> DONNA SHUGAR, ROBERTS CREEK, BRITISH COLUMBIA

My husband's stepmother grew up on the prairies during the Depression when times were hard. She learned very young to make use of everything and to throw nothing out.

Even though her circumstances had changed later in life, it was difficult for her to dispose of anything that might have value or use. She would pump wash water out of her washing machine to use again, and every discarded piece of clothing would be taken apart to reuse buttons or zippers or be cut into rags for dusting or cleaning.

Each piece of foil would be reused until it fell to pieces, Chinese food containers were cleaned and filled with food to be frozen, and wrapping paper would be smoothed and folded carefully to be used once again or to line dresser drawers. Each time we visited, she would send me home with empty margarine containers, foil pie plates, Styrofoam packages, or many and sundry other items. She felt sure I would be able to use them for storage or baking or crafts, or whatever.

I never wished to hurt her feelings, so I obligingly trucked them all the way home with us to North Bay from southwestern Ontario. I did my best to find uses for the items, either in my kindergarten class or in my crafts, but the sheer number of items became impossible for me to do anything but recycle most of them.

A year after my father-in-law passed away, my husband's stepmother decided she could no longer live on her own. We prepared to move her from her home to live with her daughter. We made the seven-hour trip to spend a weekend cleaning out the house to move furniture etc. to both of our homes. A large truck was rented, as we knew the basement contained many boxes.

The next morning, we decided to start below ground level and work our way up. As we began to remove boxes from the basement, first inspecting their contents to decide which could possibly be donated to charity or discarded, we realized that the truck we had rented could have been much smaller. As each box was opened, another mound of plastic containers, Styrofoam or foil plates was discovered. Thousands! Twenty or more years of them, to be precise. All those boxes, which had consumed precious space in their closets and recreation room, were filled with no more than used containers. We attempted to donate them to local charities, but there were more than even they could use. My mother-in-law was determined that we not throw them out, so we did our best to find homes for them all, but it was simply impossible, and into the trash they went. We all decided it would be best not to pass that information on to her, as she had worked so hard to save them all those years.

We were all taught a lesson that weekend. Doing without all those years of the Depression taught our parents something we have yet to learn, that we all could live with a lot less and should try to see value in even the simplest items.

> NANCY P. DOUGLAS, SOUTH MOUNTAIN, ONTARIO

We just moved back to Canada—yes, a doctor moving *back* to Canada— and after we had packed up our house in Ann Arbor, Michigan, we borrowed a few toys from friends so our three-year-old daughter would have something to play with. But guess what she preferred? Those pegs that fit into door hinges! She named them after her pals at daycare, Lauren and Christina, and spent the next few days getting them to sleep in pretend sleeping bags, eat their meals and so on. So now, in our new house, we look at those door pegs and our big pile of toys and know which is the favourite.

> LAURA ROSENTHAL, VANCOUVER, BRITISH COLUMBIA

I am frugal. I make leftover suppers from leftover suppers already served. I mend socks. I wash (some, not all) plastic bags to reuse. I have a used baking powder tin I have labelled: "Pieces of string too small to use."

> MARJORIE NENT, DARTMOUTH, NOVA SCOTIA

My uncle chewed tobacco, and when he finished chewing, he would dry the tobacco on the window ledge. When it was dry, he would put in a pipe and smoke it. After he smoked it, he would use the ash for snuff. When he sniffed, he sneezed. And when he sneezed, he would use the snot for shoe polish. Now that's cheap.

> KEITH G. SUTCLIFFE, DARTMOUTH, NOVA SCOTIA

My grandparents, Joe and Hilda Sketchley, moved from Quill Lake, Saskatchewan, to Havelock, New Brunswick, in 1939, as defeated prairie farmers. That Depression and two world wars taught my grandmother the value of thrift, a trait she practised to her last day on earth.

In 1978, I had graduated from high school and was working as a waitress, trying to decide what to do in life, when Grammie asked if I'd like to be her travelling companion on a train trip back to Saskatchewan. I'd never made train reservations before, so I handed over $180, and she took care of the arrangements.

In her obsessive drive to save money, she decided that the two of us could share *one sleeper bed*, which was nothing more than a single bed! We spent endless nights through Quebec, Ontario and Manitoba, rocking and rolling into each other. By the way, she felt that 9 PM was an appropriate bedtime.

I really should have known better than to have trusted my grandmother's budgeting instincts, since I'd been exposed to them all my life. She never threw *anything* out that could be reused in any way. Mouldy food—no problem. She would cut off the offending piece or eat around it. I sometimes wondered if she didn't nibble a bit of it simply to get free medication! If she burned a meal or a cake, she'd eat it anyway.

Grammie was a farmer who raised chickens. Instead of buying oyster shells for her hens to eat to manufacture the hard shells their eggs needed, she had us all saving our eggshells for her to recycle through the hens. I saved eggshells for her well into my adulthood.

She never bought gift wrap in her life. Every gift she ever gave was wrapped in second-hand paper. On every Christmas morning she spent with us, she'd wait like a cat to pounce on the pile of discarded paper which we knew would wrap our birthday gifts that year. Of course, she used her pinking shears to cut out Christmas cards with which to make gift tags.

However, none of those instances of thriftiness compares with the story of the dime. I was a little girl at the time, spending a day at her house. She didn't like me playing with a dime I had and warned me repeatedly to put it away because I might lose it.

Well, I did lose it—right down my throat! I thought it was gone forever, but I was wrong. This was before Grammie had indoor plumbing, and she made me stay at her house for a few more days while she poked and prodded my waste material with a Popsicle stick (used, of course) until she victoriously retrieved the dime!

It was my dime, but it was now unquestionably hers for all her trouble!

My brother told the dime story at her wake in 1995, much to my embarrassment! However, it is one of many fond memories I have of her.

> GISELE MCKNIGHT, SUSSEX, NEW BRUNSWICK

My parents met through mutual friends at Expo '67 and hit it off. Mom lived in Montreal and Dad lived on a farm near Viscount, Saskatchewan. They corresponded for a few months, and my mom came out to Saskatchewan by train for a "meet the family" visit in September of that year.

As the train neared Watrous, Saskatchewan, where she would be met, my mom changed into her best dress. Now, this was the era of the miniskirt, but Mom insists that this was one of her longer dresses. Anyway, she was pretty shy and desperate to make a good impression on Dad's family. All went well at the station, with introductions all around, and Mom was just starting to relax when Grandma leaned over and quietly offered to "sew a flounce" onto the hem of Mom's dress for her.

Things must have picked up from there, because Mom and Dad were engaged by the end of that visit and married in the spring of 1968.

> TINA MEYER, LANGDON, ALBERTA

My family enjoyed having our maternal grandmother living with us. She was a constant source of amusement to us when we were small, and a great compassionate listener and consoler when we got older. Through it all though, she had one flaw. She hated pocket knives!

To a nine-year-old boy in rural Newfoundland in the early 1960s, that was a serious impediment on the journey to manhood. Every other male whom I knew had a pocket knife. All my buddies had one, including my first cousin. He was her grandson, too, but he had the great fortune not to live with her. Every time I managed to get a pocket knife, she would engage her grandmother's radar and, without fail, find that knife and hide it away. To this day, I have no idea where she put them. I guess someone someday may unwittingly open an attic hatch and be crushed by the deluge of rusted pocket knives.

There was one ray of hope. After yet another knife disappeared, I was absolutely livid. In an attempt to calm me down, she conceded a little and said, "When you get two numbers in your age, you can have a pocket knife."

What a golden opportunity! In just a few short weeks, I would be ten. When that great day arrived, I proudly announced that I wanted the blue, pearl-handled Barlow knife that was in Pike's store window. To my absolute shock and dismay, my grandmother calmly proclaimed that I was being a bit premature since I was ten, not eleven. Everyone knows that ten is made up of "one" and "zero," and since "zero" is nothing, it can't be a number! I was completely devastated. Yet, I vowed not to let her get the better of me. With quivering chin and very wet eyes, I stoically grinned and swore to myself I would get that knife and she would be there to witness it.

At my next birthday, I watched her as she watched me produce that same blue, pearl-handled Barlow knife that had been the focus of my attention for the past year. I opened the knife, described in vivid detail what I would be able to do with such a knife and twirled it this way and that. When I was sure that I had thoroughly impressed everyone within earshot, I deftly closed the knife with one hand, since it was not a locking-blade type. Unfortunately, I miscalculated the strength of the spring and the sharpness of the blade. As the knife closed across the palm of my hand, it nipped the fleshy pad beneath the thumb and sliced deeply. After the yelp of fright and the scream of pain, I was quickly transported to the local doctor and became the proud owner of eight neatly sewn stitches.

When I returned home, my birthday knife was missing, to my horror. Embarrassment kept me from making a scene, even though I could detect a slight smug grin on my grandmother's face. I never did find that knife, just as I never did find any of the others. It's probably just as well, since the prospect of more stitches was much less appealing than the disgrace of being knife-less at age eleven. Besides, now I had battle scars to show off, and, in retrospect, I was much more comfortable talking about that wonderful knife then actually using it.

> JOHN M. HEALEY, MOUNT PEARL, NEWFOUNDLAND

My grandmother always carried a pocket knife. I guess it might have been the feminine version of a "jack" knife. Anyway, it looked very fancy with its pretty pearl handle. She must have noticed my fascination with it, because she gave me a smaller version, about 2 inches long, for my sixth birthday. It was blue pearl. Mom rolled her eyes, Grandma shrugged her shoulders. After Mom had looked it over, she passed it back to me, still *closed!!!*

Well, when you have a new knife, it's not much use to you all clamped shut like that. My young fingers didn't have the strength to open it, so I had to use my teeth. It opened—ta-da!—and then snapped shut on my bottom lip. Dull blade, no blood, but I had to go back to my mom with the knife stuck on my face. My little knife disappeared after that.

I've owned and presumably "lost" several pocket knives over the years. Now, I sometimes carry a Swiss Army knife that my kids gave me on another birthday. I've learned to keep it on a cord attached to a belt loop so my mom can't take it from me.

> IRENE NUNWEILER, VALEMOUNT, BRITISH COLUMBIA

I've got a neighbour who's quite the mighty woodsman, and one day he was in the backyard, splitting his wood for the winter. He came to a very reluctant chunk of wood—or, as we say around here, a "junk" of wood—and after two or three whacks, he decided to "come onto her." So he raised the axe high over his head and drove it down with all his considerable might. But the clothesline was above and behind him, and the axe hooked it. Amazingly, the clothesline had enough stretch—and such was his strength—that the axe actually got quite close to the wood.

Unfortunately, the clothesline didn't break but acted like a slingshot. The axe shot back in the same direction it had come from, but at a slightly different trajectory. It hit him just above his eyes in the centre of his forehead, lifted him off the ground and drove him back about 8 or 10 feet.

I'm sure it would have killed most lesser men, but it didn't even knock him out. It did, however, cut him fairly badly; the result was not too disastrous—two black eyes, a number of stitches, a wicked headache and a great story to tell on himself. I'm just glad I'm not telling it about myself.

> DON OSBURN, BURLINGTON, NOVA SCOTIA

One day in the summer of my youth, about '71 or '72, I was at my great uncle's place. He lived and grew up in the Eastern Townships village of Fitch Bay, Quebec, near Magog. Uncle Everet was a true Luddite. No electricity, an artesian well for water, and wood for cooking and heating. One morning, I was out chopping some wood. It was cool, with the morning dew still glistening on the grass. I was chopping away, placing chunks of wood on a big chopping block, usually taking one or two good swings to split the chunks.

There was this one big piece, the size of a 5-gallon pail. I knew it would be a bit tough. I raised the axe as high as I could, bringing down a mighty swing. The axe stopped just short of the piece of wood.

I stared and stood straight up, thinking: what's not right here? Did I mention that I was standing under the clothesline while doing this? The axe had caught on the clothesline and came swinging back straight at me. Right between the eyes!

I raised my hand to my face and it came back red with blood. I screamed, dropped the axe and went running into the house. My poor mother didn't know whether to scream or laugh. Once they realized what had happened, they all started laughing, myself included.

Uncle Everet said, "Good thing that wasn't a two-headed axe!"

> R.D.

My Grannie Bell taught me to chop wood. She came over from a small family farm in Scotland in the early years of the last century and was tight-fisted enough to make my miner-grandfather's dream of owning a farm come true. They only had two children, both of whom they wanted in school, so Grannie Bell became Grandpa's chief hand in the running of those thin-soiled Canadian Shield acres. After miner's lung took Grandpa, Grannie ran the farm on her own for about a dozen years.

She was extremely comfortable with an axe in her hands by the time she bullied her way into her eighties and started spending winters with us "in city." Many an early-dark winter evening, my brother and I would be sinking deeply into the family couch in front of the television, when Grannie would march in from the masses of pots she always had bubbling on the stove and declare in a sergeant's voice, "Wae naed wud fir tha faere! Whoo'll chop't? Mm? Whoo'll chop tha wud?" Of course, she'd stand and wait for a reply, and, of course, we'd ignore her until she left, shaking her head in disgust as she went, tottering and muttering, out through the kitchen and the garage to the woodpile—which was located directly on the other side of the wall from the couch on which my brother and I sat, teeth clenched, awaiting the thuds. And soon they'd come: Thud...THUD...thud. THUD...thud...THUD.

We knew one of us had to go out there and take over the chopping, not because Grannie was unable but because we knew that if one of us didn't get out there soon, she'd have the work done *and* the load of wood delivered to the fireplace in the room where we sat. Then it was the wrath of Dad we'd face, and righteous is the wrath of a man whose teenage sons let his eighty-plus-year-old mother chop the firewood.

So, off I'd go to wrestle the axe from Grannie and assure her that I knew how to handle it. She always watched me for a few minutes, offering sharp-brogued assessments of everything I was doing wrong. I always chafed under a supervision I deemed both humiliating and unnecessary. However, I did learn to chop wood, and whenever I'm lucky enough to be chopping wood now, I smile to think that Grannie Bell is probably elbowing God and muttering, "Hae's still swinging tew harde. Dae yew nae thinke hae's still swinging tew harde?"

> D.B.

My grandmother was a very large and buxom woman. As a child I would watch with fascination, and later, when I was older, with horror, as she bound herself into a corset each morning. The result was a rock hard, solid chest that would probably make any comic book hero jealous of her ability to repel any flying object by simply asserting her chest! I was snuggled, rocked and hugged against that wall of flesh until I was twenty-five. It smelled of face powder that fell off the puff and Avon soaps and perfumes. It provided warmth, strength, security and love. Enter the fur coat.

Every November, Grandma would take out her fur coat to provide her with warmth during the Remembrance Day parade (my grandfather was a WWI veteran). I can remember many a cold parade at which she held me against her fur coat to keep me warm. In the car travelling, she would always let you cuddle up in its warmth. Christmas Eve, I would fall asleep against it on the way home from midnight mass. It was soft and warm and had a certain smell to it, but the thing I remember most is that despite its thick layer of softness, beneath it lay the solid bosom which gave me love, security and comfort for most of my life.

I am a small person, and Grandma's fur would wrap around me at least twice. When my mother gave me Grandma's coat, she encouraged me to trade it for another coat or to have it altered. I could not do that because it was Grandma's coat.

Although Grandma has been gone for fifteen years, her coat still has that warmth and the smell of her. Sometimes I run my fingers through it and quickly remember that we were not allowed to do that as children. However, when times are bad due to one or another of life's many knocks, I cuddle on the couch with that coat. I hold it to my face and feel my grandmother's solidness beneath its surface and am reminded of all of the good things in life, mostly of all the love and the special people in my life, and I feel better.

> M.F.

In the cold snap of 1970-something, Stephen and I went to the Three Vets store to buy him a winter coat. He'd come to the balmy west coast from Toronto, leaving all his warm clothing behind. We settled on an olive drab WWII army greatcoat. It came down to his ankles, weighed a ton, and, in retrospect, with his slight frame, he looked like a refugee wearing it.

It had snowed, partly melted and then frozen hard. The sidewalks were lumpy with ice and treacherous. My black leather knee-high boots had no tread. I slipped and fell a number of times as we headed back to my cold-water flat to smoke a joint and play a few tunes. We speculated on the previous owner of the greatcoat. Was he alive or dead? Where had he served? Had the coat been warm enough or just heavy and cumbersome? Stephen and his partner disappeared into the night, leaving me to finish the bottle of wine I'd opened and crawl into bed.

I came down with the flu. I vaguely remember my parents coming by and bringing me a blue electric blanket. I tuned them out. I was so sick that I awoke one morning unable to open my eyes. They were glued shut by a sticky discharge. I had to boil a kettle to get warm water to bathe them. Stephen and his partner came by later that day with chicken soup. They had made it themselves from a packaged mix. They sat on the end of my bed, watching me eat it. We could see our breath, it was so cold in the room. I told them how to light the oil space heater, which they eventually managed to do as I coached them from my sickbed. I was coughing, so I passed on the joint they were sharing. They came by every day for a week with food, trying to coax me to eat delicacies like pâté and halvah, Greek olives and doggy bagged dim sum. They knew I was feeling better when I got up and made them a pot of peppermint tea, which we drank with the joint they had lit up.

Was it ten years later, fifteen, when I got the letter from Stephen's mother? She had been going through her son's effects some time after he died of AIDS. She'd found the greatcoat and wondered about it. And this is where memory fails me. Did she find the ten-dollar bill in an inside pocket, or was it Stephen who found it when I visited him in Toronto in 1983?

My story could diverge here. I could say that Stephen and I took the ten-dollar bill and bought a live chicken in Kensington Market, went away to do some other shopping while it was butchered and later took it to his parents' place, where he cooked me the tastiest chicken dinner I'd ever had. I could recall how I cleaned the mould out of his parents' dishwasher—they'd been away a few weeks—and changed the stinking kitty litter defiled by Vicious and Precious, the two Siamese cats (housekeeping was never one of Stephen's strong suits).

Or, maybe it was his mother who found the ten spot as she searched his belongings for clues to her son's life. In any case, I wrote her a long letter about the winter Stephen had bought the coat. How he and his partner had nursed me through my flu. How we used to meander around Chinatown, buying trinkets, have dim sum and end up back at my place playing music.

I figured that by that time, the original owner of the greatcoat was most likely dead. But what did I know? Maybe he's still alive and has outlived Stephen, my once and future best friend.

> JANET BICKFORD, VANCOUVER, BRITISH COLUMBIA

Twelve years ago, my husband and I, along with our three children, moved to the Ottawa area. Our oldest child, a son, was fourteen at the time and had recently discovered the fun of curling. He had searched diligently for many years to find a sport he could both enjoy and be really good at. He was never one to let anything get in his way, though sometimes your health can dictate events.

For several years, life was as you would expect with three children. Our son progressed on in his curling and in 1990 became the skip of his junior curling team. Aha, he thought, I've arrived. That fall, in late October, he was hospitalized for what we all thought would be a routine treatment of antibiotics, as is common for most people with cystic fibrosis. Two days before his release, he spiked a temperature and, as they say, all hell broke loose. We were told that at sixteen years of age, his time was up, and we had only a few more weeks to spend with him.

On Sunday, his team was to curl a game, and he was determined to go. We tried to talk him out of this, but no, he was going. Well, we were very worried, because, you see, at this time he weighed around 70 pounds and the curling rocks are 40 or so pounds, and it can be very cold on the ice.

We went to the rink.

The game was not going well—the team needed to win to finish the round in first place, and in his mind that's where his team belonged. As the game progressed into the sixth end, people began to gather around his father and me back behind the glass as we watched what was turning out to be a very frustrating experience for him and for us.

It was at this point that my heart broke, because he turned around to us, and, with the most despairing look on his face, he mouthed, "I can't get the rock over the hog line." To any curler, this is most frustrating and embarrassing.

In the seventh end, people were beginning to realize that the slim blond warrior on the ice was probably playing his last game before waging one final battle with his disease.

In the eighth end, he was down one point, and skip rocks for both teams were all that were left. With his first rock, he buried it and made it count, and with his second, he won the game. There were no dry eyes as he gave us all one huge grin. Someone said, "Damn good for you," and it was.

I wish I could say he won his battle with cystic fibrosis, but he died five days later. When he curled, he wore a big baggy grey sweater and colourful jacket to try to keep warm. I inherited that sweater and wear it when I curl— it's been ten years, and the sweater that warmed his body now warms my heart and keeps him ever close.

> GENNY PAYN, KINGSTON, ONTARIO

I could hardly wait for March. I dug out last year's jacket, and it mostly fit. I didn't waste time zipping it.

Outside, the sunshine was thinner than I had expected, and the wind brisker. I poked a stick into mud and grass and last year's wasp nest. I gaped at the pale sky, and my hair blew into my mouth. My hair tasted of sun and wind. I turned the stick around and around. It wasn't straight, and twigs snagged out of it like teeth, but it would do. I snapped it in two and ran inside, but not because I was cold.

With paper and crayons and glue and string and my two sticks, I made a kite. As long as I ran and kept the string short, the kite didn't bump along the ground, but flew straight out behind me.

And then, one evening before dinner, my father took us down the hill to the drugstore to choose a kite. We agreed on red, if they had it, purple if they didn't, or blue, which, by then, had faded to purple, anyway, on the drugstore's shelves.

That night, dinner just had to be something I hated, like pea soup, something thick and pasty that could not possibly be swallowed before dark. My brother gobbled his dinner and assembled the kite. My mother tore up rags and constructed a tail. My father searched the basement for the string on the wooden reel that he'd made another year. My sister and I stirred spoons through congealing soup. Tears gathered in my eyes.

My sister finished her soup and put on her boots!

My father and brother zipped their jackets!

I choked down the last spoonful, stumbled into my boots, grabbed my jacket, left our mother behind with the dishes and pounded up the hill, sobbing, "Wait for me!"

One street away, Crawford's Hill rose baldly to the sky. Dried, buff-coloured grasses grew from spiky, broken-off tufts of the year before's grasses. When it was my turn, the kite flew up into the wind and danced in the sky. It waggled its tail, bright with torn-up dresses and shirts. It tugged at the string in my hands. And then ... I was not on the ground. I was floating in the sky. I was looking down at myself and at my sister and my brother and my father, and we were all tiny.

The kite dipped toward earth.

Everyone yelled, "Pull it up!" I pulled and I pulled, but I wasn't really in the sky, I couldn't pull it up. I was on the ground, and could only pull it down ... It looped up, then whirled and tumbled in larger and larger circles. It was going to land, I knew it was going to land! And I knew where it was going to land. Crawford's Hill was bald, except for one thicket of trees. The kite settled too high for my father to reach it. The trees were too fragile for us to climb. The sky had gone that funny shade that was neither blue nor lavender nor pink, the colour that reminds you to find the first star so you can make a wish. My father took out his pocket knife and cut the string.

Silently, I offered my apologies to our torn kite with its tangled, twisted tail, and I thought I saw the crossbars of last year's kite dangling from the same tree.

> JANET BOLIN, MOUNT VERNON, NEW YORK

The year was 1966, the place was Yarbo, Saskatchewan. My best friend, Lyn, and I were twelve years old. During the bimonthly gathering of our two families, we were driving our parents nuts with our continual complaints of boredom. Finally, they told us to go fly a kite. April was still the middle of winter in Saskatchewan, so we inquired, sarcastically, "Where?"

"On the moon," one of them replied in desperation.

We decided to show them. We wrote a letter to Lyndon B. Johnson. It took a long time, but we did get a reply, not from the president, who likely had better things to do, but from Charles A. Anderson, United States Vice Consul.

He wrote: "The first colony on the moon will not be set up for at least another thirty-four years. It would be premature, therefore, to send you tickets to the moon at this time. Because all of the first group of 'passengers' to the moon will have to be scientists, I would suggest that, in order to qualify for the first moon colony, you begin working towards a Ph.D. degree in Astro-physics."

I kept the letter and have let my kids make fun of me over the years about this incredible thing their mother and friend did. By the way, neither of us attempted to gain a Ph.D. in Astro-physics.

> C.H.

Spring was ushered into our home on the bottom of my daughter's snow boot. The melting snow had yielded up its seasonal accumulation of our darling Brittany spaniel's poop.

Sticking the boot into the toilet to soak—a great tip from a friend that saves a lot of nasty scraping, though one must remember to remove the boot, for, in our experience, it is sure to startle unsuspecting guests—I armed myself with the designated "poop patrol" shovel.

It is a mystery to me why this chore is viewed with such delight by children, but my little entourage soon consisted not only of my own two but of four neighbouring ones. And so I spent a miserable two hours trudging across the yard. The kids selected for themselves the job of locating the material in question, with much jumping up and down and shouting. Several children were old enough to have picked up some delightful bathroom jokes at school, and this was viewed as the perfect opportunity to share them with their younger friends. It is a peculiarity of small children that they seem to find that a joke gets funnier the more times it is told. I was unable to share this view and focussed on the job at hand, working hard to dispel the urge to scoop the children up on the shovel and fling them down the ravine to join the objects of their hilarity.

At last, even their keen young eyes could find no more, and they settled down on the driveway with a box of chalk. I leaned on the shovel, with a bland sense of accomplishment. Ours was a poop-free property. To top off this accomplishment, I decided that today was the day to take down the Christmas lights. This, too, is a spring tradition for us. We have a gently slopping roof, and, if you wait until the snow has melted off it and pick an early sunny afternoon, it is most delightful to scoot along above the eavestroughs, unclipping the lights from the gutter. What chore could be more removed from the unpleasant mucky task just completed? Up there it would be just me, the warm tar shingles, the beautiful town and mountain vista, with the laughing voices of the children as they played below. Perfect.

I dragged the ladder out of the garage and scrambled up, enjoying as always the delightful sensations of daring adventure and whispering vertigo, of the weirdness of being on the roof. And then I saw it. My brain rebelled against it, but to no avail. There it sat, alone on the unbroken expanse of sandpapery shingles. A little pile of poop, artistically centred near the crest. On the roof.

The explanation was not long in dawning. My mind drew up a vision of our cat, who last year had mastered the art of making the jump from porch rail to roof. There, she spent many a summer evening soaking in the warmth of the blacktop, delightfully out of reach of the pesky dog. I could picture her now, in the depth of winter, making the leap up onto a roof covered in a blanket of snow, happily digging her hole in this deep white blanket and later covering it carefully over again, content.

> MARGARET HAMPSHIRE, TERRACE, BRITISH COLUMBIA

Mᵧ household consists of five people: two adults and three school-age children. An unwavering sign of spring for me is the sudden and dramatic increase in footwear at every entry to the house. Spring is an unreliable beast, so the snow boots must remain at the ready. This is Ottawa, after all, and the possibility of one last bitter snowstorm or cold spell is not to be dismissed. And rain boots are required for the March showers, never mind the more familiar April ones. And, since I finally weakened to the daily cry of "Mom, can we please get our bikes out today?" running shoes have been present, too.

Yes, the foot attire is as pervasive as Canada geese in an unplowed corn field at migration time; and, like the geese, much of this gear is migrating, too. In addition to the snow boots, there are skates and cross-country ski

192

boots waiting for their annual voyage south to the basement. Other items have only just arrived; they will spend their summer here. These include adult jogging shoes. Those spring days characterized by strong sun and unseasonably warm temperatures demand that we cast aside our lost enthusiasms of winter and begin "the program" yet again. And although spring temperatures can still leave bare tootsies a mite uncomfortable, I confess there is a pair of summer sandals already peeking out from behind the back door. After all, when running late to meet the school bus, it is infinitely faster to shove something on your feet that do not require bending over.

How many boots or shoes adorn my doorways? Today's count was forty-seven. There appears to be a snow boot missing. From past experience, I am confident that this lone item will find its way home only at the end of June, when school is out and children are sent home with all manner of wayward bits and pieces. But I never will solve the mystery of how Joe's left foot got home safely on that last winter day.

> ANNE WRIGHT, GLOUCESTER, ONTARIO

T he river fishing boots which come up to your chest and fasten like coveralls are called "waders." The old ones were big, heavy and dangerous if they filled accidentally. You could do almost the same job with "hip boots," which though also clunky and ill-fitting, are shorter and aren't joined at the top. They hook into your belt with small loops, and so are much easier to jettison should the need arise. And you keep your pants on. That's what Dad always used, and I got them when he died last year.

My dad's eighty-six years began in a small Midwestern parsonage and ended in a care facility across the street from his house in Port Angeles, Washington. We children and a lot of other relatives gathered for some tender, sad and humorous days, remembering Dad with formal gatherings and informal conversations. The family is large, and he left vivid memories with his strong personality cast in the role of a small-town doctor. Toward the end of his practice, he delivered some of his first babies' grandchildren.

He left a lot of personal gear in boxes and closets. We were gathered in part to distribute it, in a process which is also the beginning steps of our new family life without Papa. There were shotguns and tackle boxes, paintings, photographs and old office equipment, duplicated and reduplicated tools, furniture and books, kitchen gadgets, silly little birthday presents from long ago, pocket knives, Bibles, pills, letters home from summer camp and his Coast Guard enlistment papers. His stuff.

And clothes, quite a pile as Papa seldom threw anything out. At the end, he had nearly two hundred bow ties, lots of hats, bathrobes, winter jackets and old suits. And shoes. Since I had inherited his big feet, I got his shoes. Most went on the donation pile, but not his old hip boots.

Pulling them out of the box let loose a terrible odour, a mix of old sweat-soaked rubber, mildew and dried fish slime. The weaker children quickly cleared the room, leaving a couple of brothers and me to savour a smell that took us back to "o-dark-thirty" departures and long rainy days on the river, fishing with Papa.

I took them outside and hung them on the line, filled each with warm water and a cup or two of bleach and then turned them upside down, rinsed them and left them to dry in the wind. Papa's boots.

My brother got the only photograph of him wearing the boots. He's got this magnificent grin and is holding up six steelhead. They're big, most over twenty pounds, and are strung along a pole. Bob, his fishing partner, holds the other end.

Looking at the boots, cleaning them, and especially wearing them fishing, brings back dimensions of being with Papa on the river I never realized I knew. At the time, I was usually impatient, frequently cold and always hungry. Now this outdated gear makes me walk the riverbanks and shallows with the same careful waddle Papa used to use. For a couple of hundred dollars, I could get the latest breathable waders with felt soles and dance across the wet and slippery rocks, but somehow this is better, at least for a while. I still slip sometimes and fill them with river water, and, as we did then, I usually just continue sloshing around, waiting for the water to warm up, keeping my fly on the water.

These were the boots he wore when he caught those giant steelhead in the photo. The ones he had on when I saw him trip and go into the river well over his head, losing his glasses and scaring me silly. The ones he wore when he missed another big fish his partner was playing, finally poking himself in the leg with the gaff. The quarter-sized patch is still there, still watertight. His partner got him a new gaff for his birthday later that year, with a miniature hangman's noose on the handle. "One end's for the fish," he began.

Papa's boots are a treasure because they're as much a part of who he was as his moustache and of what we once enjoyed doing together as a personal, handwritten note. The smell has faded, as will the memories, but until then, it's the kind of thing that brings Dad closer, a legacy of himself, what he was like to be with and what we shared when he was healthy and I was young.

> JACK KINTER (ALREADY A CBC LISTENER WHEN DIEFENBAKER WAS
ELECTED THE FIRST TIME), BLAINE, WASHINGTON

When my parents and grandparents fled as refugees from the Nazis, they were allowed to take only the tiniest sum of money with them. Their apartments and businesses were confiscated and the furniture they sold for a pittance, since the buyers had all the power. What they could do was ship their smaller stuff overseas. This is why I spent my childhood in a house full of fine silver tea services, coloured crystal goblets that held the longest purest chime, vases, linen tea towels, dolls, jewellery, paintings, leather-bound classics and the preposterous eyelet-embroidered bloomers of my grandmother's trousseau (made for a giantess, although she was four-foot ten).

In my almost six decades of traipsing about a perfectly peaceful North America, I have lost, broken or otherwise parted with more stuff than I can name, yet my mother still lives with much of that rescued stuff. (She does lament the things she did lose: the six years of correspondence with my father in which they practised their new language and told each other about their lives—hers as a maid, waitress and clerk in England, and his as an American soldier—thrown out by a landlord who stole the trunk they were stored in.) As she gets older, I wonder how we, her descendants, will continue to honour these things.

I live in a single room with too much stuff already, my brother has a tiny flat in London (U.K.), and my son has taken over the "homestead" I carved out of the B.C. bush in the '70s. He is mostly concerned with housing his snowboards, dirt bikes and fishing gear. I don't see crystal goblets in his "lifestyle."

Of course, my parents weren't content to be stewards of the rescued treasures but set about adding to them once they could afford it. I feel responsible for the care of the trove. Even things that are not to my taste have stepped beyond such considerations and become as close as family. I am sure that there are others like me and that a solution can be found in *Roundup* land. We need to find people who can appreciate such objects and their history. I sometimes envy those who, after a fire or robbery, could replace their goods with a few 800 calls to the shopping channel.

> ANNE SCHMITZ, OTTAWA, ONTARIO

In 1913, Dad decided he would build a round barn on our family farm. I remember him spending hours drawing up a floor plan and designing the barn himself. He bought two cement-block moulds, one for the barn, the other for the silo. The silo blocks were slightly curved, and the ones for the barn were rectangular. We hauled sand for the cement from a nearby bluff.

Making these blocks was a tough job. It took four people about fifteen minutes to make each block. So we were all very pleased on the day Dad announced that we had enough blocks to begin building.

Dad cut most of the wood for the barn's frame from trees on the farm. However, he hauled the boards for the sides and the hay floor from town with our two workhorses, Dan and Fox.

Some local men helped to build the barn. The ones I remember are Martin, Will and Norman Roth, Louis Schuett, Happy Gibler and Shark Pharo. Frank Steiner put on the tin roof and made the cupola.

When Frank and Dad erected the lightning rod on top of the cupola, they forgot to put the ball on its upper end. Rather than take the rod down again, Dad stood on Frank's shoulders, way up on the roof, and slipped the ball on the rod. The barn had fifteen bents, 15 feet each. It also had a basement 10 feet deep and 72 feet in diameter. The silo, at 14 by 38 feet, held 128 tons of silage.

When the barn was finished in 1915, Dad was understandably proud. It was not only beautiful but also well braced and constructed. Because it was round, with the silo in the centre, feeding the cattle was about as easy as it could be. Before putting hay in the barn, we held a dance to celebrate its completion. Guests arrived in about sixty carriages. Our neighbours, the McEvoys, were the first to arrive. They tied their horses to the pine tree just west of the house. In those days, everyone brought a lantern and some cake to a dance. The lanterns were hung inside for light.

Fred Potter and his wife were the "orchestra" that night. He played the fiddle, and she played the organ. When I asked Dad how long he thought the barn would last, he said, "Eighty years."

Well, he came close to being right. The present owners of the land, who had no use for the barn, decided to burn it down to make room for crops. My wife and I watched the old barn disappear in flames and smoke seventy-eight years after it was built. Now, the land where it stood is used for growing crops. It looks pretty much like it did back when Dad first got the idea to build a round barn.

(This barn story was written by my dad, Bill Walsh, in 1994. He was a man with a remarkable memory. He died in 1999, nine days short of his ninetieth birthday. The barn was located near Mauston, Wisconsin.)

> PATRICIA FORNELLI, VANCOUVER, BRITISH COLUMBIA

I have some glowing (if rather hazy) memories of performances and parties at the Atlantic Folk Festival at Hardwoodlands in Nova Scotia in the late '70s and early '80s. Many more special memories come from the Newfoundland and Labrador Folk Festival here in St. John's. I met my husband backstage at the 1990 festival: by the time the 1991 festival rolled around, we had just discovered that I was pregnant with our first child. I used to say that, after meeting Pius almost on the stage, I didn't dare sing again for fear of what else would happen to me; but when he was diagnosed with inoperable cancer, he suggested that, in three or four years' time, I should try to get on stage again and see if I couldn't get another fellow. (I haven't done it yet.)

But I want to tell you about what happened at the Burin Peninsula Folk Arts Festival. It's been taking place in Burin on the first weekend of July for fifteen years now. Most of the performers either live or have lived on the Burin Peninsula; many come from communities that disappeared during that period of government-sponsored dislocation colloquially known as "resettlement times."

The emphasis at Burin is on the styles of performance that have been traditional in Newfoundland communities. Electric instruments are rarely heard, for example, and many of the singers are unaccompanied. The festival organizers can pay some travel expenses, but performers themselves usually appear for free—even those professional musicians who have discovered the festival.

What draws performers back year after year is the experience of seeing and hearing and performing with people for whom this music is an expression of their soul. One set in particular generates that feeling every year. It's called "Out of Placentia Bay," because its performers have all left the communities they "belonged to," as the saying goes here, either because of resettlement or for other pressing reasons. There are usually ten or twelve people on the stage—singers, step dancers, accordion players and a scattered miscellany of others. Most of them know each other, and the stage takes on the atmosphere of a kitchen party as singers join with whoever is singing and dancers are drawn from their seats by the relentless drive of a jig played in a style (and at a pace!) that could come only from a Newfoundlander's instrument.

For the people on that stage—and for many in the audience—sessions like these were part of the experience not just of family but of community life from the time they were children. For most young Newfoundlanders, these kinds of experiences are now available only in the context of a public performance. My husband and I made a point of taking the children to the Burin Festival and letting them loose amongst the performers backstage to listen to songs or dance to the music of the impromptu combos that spring up at that kind of event. For Pius, this had the resonance of childhood experience. Since his death, it's the power of the music that draws me back year after year, and gives both context and community to the songs the children and I sing and listen to every day and to the stories I tell them about their father.

They have a tradition at the Burin Festival of placing empty chairs on the stage in memory of festival participants who have died during the year. I have wept at the sight of the empty chair of my father-in-law, a noted Placentia Bay singer and storyteller. I have sung on the stage with my husband's empty chair in the wings behind me.

Over the years, there have been a lot of empty chairs in the set that is "Out of Placentia Bay," but this year, they stuck in an extra chair at the last minute. My son, John Pius, is six years old. Ever since he was born, he has heard the old songs—from his grandfather as long as he was alive; from his father while we

199

still had him; from his older sister's mother, herself a noted traditional singer who takes a great interest in him; and from me. John Pius knows a lot of songs, but he's usually reluctant to let anyone hear him sing them.

This year, with some tactful encouragement from Anita, he took his place beside her in the Placentia Bay set. He sat there under the lights of the stage, his feet swinging well above the floor as he watched the dancers and listened to the other singers. It happened that he knew some of the songs the others sang, so he would join in from time to time. When his turn came, he sang "Jim Harris," a song about an incident involving a well-known Placentia Bay sea captain.

One of the hardest things my husband had to face when he was dying was the fear that the line of tradition bearers stretching back through him to his father, his grandfather and beyond, might end with his own death—that the chairs might always remain empty. I think there were other people in the audience that night who heard my son introduced—he has the same name as his father and grandfather—and wept to see the chair being filled again.

The set finished with a rousing accordion tune that brought all the men on stage to their feet. John Pius sat and watched for a moment, then stood at the edge of the stage, trying to decide whether he would join in. After some hesitation, his feet began to move. One of the dancers noticed, and they opened their circle to bring him in. I watched my little boy dancing with the men in the place where his father had danced before him, and I cried.

> MARY ELLEN WRIGHT, ST. JOHN'S, NEWFOUNDLAND